GOD CAN MOVE MOUNTAINS

The Story of the Christian Appalachian Project

by
Father Ralph W. Beiting

with
Constance Clark

When I began my mountain journey as a young man, many people deeply influenced my life, instilling it with hope and perseverance and stirring in me the desire to serve God through his people.

As nearly 40 years have passed, many wonderful people have come along, and with loving generosity, made it possible for me to continue to grow in His service. Through the prayer and sacrifice of supporting friends, my journey is as exciting today as it has been at any time in the past.

I would like to dedicate this book to all of them, especially to Ralph and Martha Beiting, my parents, who for more than 30 years shared in the joy and pain of the Christian Appalachian Project through their love, support and hard work.

To my ten brothers and sisters, their families and all the countless brothers and sisters in Christ, whose love has strengthened my way, I give humble thanks.

I hope the beauty this book contains will reflect on all these men and women who have supported and inspired me.

May the good God, who keeps better count of these things than I, bless them and keep them always in the palm of His hand.

—Father Ralph W. Beiting

TABLE OF CONTENTS

PROLOGUE

When I first met Cecil, I almost couldn't believe that anybody could live in such blackness — not for a day, and certainly not for 10 long, lonely years.

But Cecil was living proof of just how much a human being can endure.

To meet Cecil, you have to run a kind of obstacle course.

First, you must travel deep into the mountains of eastern Kentucky, past a little town called Martin and into a remote and narrow valley between two mountains.

This valley is called a "holler," and it is in places like this that the poor of eastern Kentucky cling to life.

Once you've snaked up the holler on a slippery mud road to where Cecil lives, you park your car wherever you can. Then you must cross a creek, picking your way carefully over a footbridge whose deck is made of two narrow boards.

The bridge hangs about 10 feet up over the creek, and it's a good 40 feet long. In case you need to hold on for balance — as I did — there's a thin wire cable that might give you some stability.

The bridge swings in the winter wind. It gets icy. It's not safe.

But Cecil must walk the bridge to get to his coal supply, dumped at the side of the road every so often.

Cecil is eighty-three years old. His eyesight is pretty bad. And, though he gets around, his walk is stiff and uncertain.

A fall from the bridge would surely kill Cecil.

But it would also kill him not to have the coal to burn.

So Cecil crosses the bridge. It's a death-defying act. Cecil specializes in defying the odds.

Once across the bridge, you see an old frame farmhouse that once boasted a wide, beautiful front porch. There Cecil and his parents and brothers must have had many happy hours together as a family.

But now, Cecil is all alone in the house. He lives in the one room that is still even remotely habitable. The rest of the house is closed off, literally falling down around the old man.

You bang on Cecil's door, which long since lost its hinges. It takes him a while to come to open it. You hear him moving things away from the door — the things he props up against it to lock out danger. (Believe it or not, Cecil was robbed not too long ago.) Finally, he opens the door.

There stands a short little man who looks to be completely black, except for his startling blue eyes. He's wearing a stocking cap and several layers of old, black clothes. After a minute, you realize his beard and hair are not *quite* black. They might be white, or gray, under the layers of coal dust.

Cecil was hospitable, inviting me in to sit for a while.

Except for the glow from a single light bulb hanging from the middle of the ceiling, Cecil's room was black.

The walls were black, with old paper peeling away from the corners and hanging in huge black curls. The cardboard stuck in the holes in the wall — Cecil's attempt to patch the crumbling house — was black. The coal stove in the middle of the room was black, with the brand name "FATSO" written across the top of it. The quilt on the bed showed a faint patchwork pattern under a strong film of black.

Even Cecil's cat — his only companion — barely showed his orange-and-white tabby markings.

Every single thing in the room, including Cecil, carried a thick layer of the residue you get when you burn coal in a badly ventilated place.

Cecil didn't have much choice other than to get black and stay black.

You see, he has no running water, no toilet facilities. He has to go out back and haul water from a well to wash. When you're all alone, and your bones ache, and it's cold, and nobody's going to see you anyway, you lose interest in washing off the coal grime.

And when it's a struggle just to heat up a can of beans on top of the coal stove called "FATSO," you're not exactly worrying about getting your spring cleaning done.

It's hard to imagine the depth of Cecil's loneliness.

For 10 years, the only people who knew he was there were his brother and sister-in-law, who live a good two hours' drive away.

They bring Cecil food once a month. But they're in no position to take him in, or find him more adequate lodging, even if Cecil wanted to go.

For 10 years, their monthly visit was all the company Cecil knew. Then one day, a lady who lived down the road happened to catch a glimpse of him as he came out to his coal pile.

She alerted one of our Christian Appalachian Project workers, and we paid a call on Cecil. We brought him some good-quality used clothes. And we set about to find out what else we could do for him.

We got to know the man and his story. It seems Cecil sank slowly into loneliness and despair as, one by one, his beloved family members moved away or died. The family homestead is the one thing he has left, and he wants to stay there. Somehow he has come to accept his isolation as a way of life.

In our day, it's hard to imagine: no phone, no T.V., not even a radio, no close neighbors, nothing to break the monotony and the desolation of poverty and old age in the mountains.

Cecil is a good, kind man. He's shy and reserved, perhaps from living so many years alone.

I don't know if he trusts us yet. But we're working on building a friendship with him.

In fact, we're building more than that.

Through our Home Repair Program, we have built Cecil a new house, right next to his beloved family home. The house is tiny — just one room, no bigger than most living rooms — but it has electric heat and sound wiring, solid walls and windows, and, best of all, running water and a bathroom.

I went to visit Cecil just before Christmas. For Cecil in recent years, Christmas hasn't meant much. But this year he had a lot to look forward to.

We brought him a Christmas basket full of good food and some new things to wear. And our staff gave him a special present — an inexpensive pocket watch on a chain. I wish you could have seen his face as he unwrapped and gazed at his new watch!

When I visited, the crew had completed his modest little house except for painting and some other finishing touches. Cecil was still holed up in his old room, burning the coal stove hard as it could go to keep warm, standing in front of it with his hands extended over its glow.

He offered to show me his new house. I only wish the CAP donors who made it possible for us to give Cecil this gift could have witnessed Cecil's intense pride as he picked up his key and walked me over to the new abode.

He turned the shiny new key in the lock, took me in, and showed around his tiny dwelling.

Cecil and I are friends now. I thank God for His great grace in transforming this lonely, desolate life into one of hope. At last, deep in the mountains, the love of good people — the love of God — has touched his life.

Already, Cecil is out of the darkness, living in a new light.

And bringing light into darkness is what the Christian Appalachian Project is all about.

The Floods

As long as earth endures: seed-time and harvest, cold and heat, summer and winter, day and night will never cease.

— Genesis 8:22
(The Lord speaks to Noah after the flood.)

The Bible doesn't tell us what the world looked like once those mighty flood waters receded. I wonder how Noah felt, surveying the damage.

When you've seen a flood's devastation first-hand, it really brings home to you just how great a promise the Lord made to Noah with the rainbow.

In the aftermath of one of eastern Kentucky's worst floods, a 75-year-old mountain woman named Sadie sat on her front porch, watching her daughter haul away ruined belongings — all the earthly possessions her little family had managed to scrape together, now mostly ruined by flood waters.

I asked Sadie if she would move away. I guess I thought this flood might have broken her spirit.

"No, I'll not move away," she stated firmly. "My children, they want me to move away. They want me to go to Lexington where there won't be any floods."

She looked around her, at the still-swollen, muddy creek, at the hills that seem to rise almost straight up from the holler's floor.

"But I can't go to Lexington or Middlesboro, or some far off place like that," she continued. In a face deeply lined with the wear of years, her eyes still shone with a spirited energy.

"You see over there on that hill?" She pointed across the creek. "My man lies buried over there. I can't move away from him. We were married for more than 40 years. My children were born and raised in this house."

I looked around the little house. I watched the daughter carry away another armful of sodden, ruined belongings. It had taken them a lifetime to save up the money to buy these few things — a couple of cheap chairs, a mattress, some clothes, maybe a few treasured knickknacks. It took the flood only a few short hours to destroy all of it. At least the house was still standing — and these people were alive.

"I've got too much here to leave," Sadie told me.

"How will you make it?" I asked.

"God is still here. He didn't get washed away in the flood and if He's still here then I know I can make it."

That's the kind of faith these mountain people have. It's the kind of faith I try to have as I live and work among them. It helps them keep on going, in spite of floods and house fires and poverty and misery of a kind rarely seen in the rest of these United States.

Bad floods are just a part of life in eastern Kentucky. They come regularly, at least once every ten years, usually more often. They are a natural consequence of heavy spring rain in the mountains. Every creek swells to bursting and races down from mountaintop to holler with the force of a massive river. City streets become canals, hollers become reservoirs, fields become lakes.

The little houses the people live in here are often no more than shacks. They're built up against the sides of mountains or in the precious little flatland between the mountain ridges. They're made of scrap wood and tarpaper precariously put together. If there's plumbing, it's often primitive. The people do the best they can with what they have, which isn't much.

These houses can't stand up to the flood waters that sweep through the hollers. Even when the structures remain intact, mud and silt destroy furniture, clothing, appliances — anything in their path. After the flood, dampness combines with haphazard electrical wiring, causing fires. As so often happens in these mountains, one disaster follows another.

When the floods come, the Christian Appalachian Project reacts instantly. We've been victims of the floods, too. Our buildings, our programs can be swept away in the first day of a bad flood.

But the staff people and the volunteers of CAP don't have time to worry about "our" precious projects when a flood comes. We're too busy trying to save the lives of our friends. And once we've done what we can to ensure their safety, we must help them find new homes and clothes and furniture and food.

One thing we never need to give them is the spirit of survival. They've gotten that from living in these mountains for generations. And they need it, for this is not an easy place to live.

God gave eastern Kentucky an abundance of natural beauty — wooded mountains, clear flowing streams and rivers, lush green valleys. I have never seen a more beautiful place than these mountains in the spring, when wildflowers burst from dark crevices in the rock, or in the autumn, when the trees display every glorious hue of yellow, red, and orange, like a brilliant sunset painted on the hills.

This land was also endowed with riches in the form of minerals — most notably coal — and timber. So why is it one of the poorest regions in the United States?

Why do fewer people graduate from high school in eastern Kentucky than anywhere in America?

Why do the children still go hungry? Why do the grown men bend over in despair halfway through their lives, forsaking the prospect of making a life for themselves?

The answers to those questions are complex. Simply put, the stark poverty of Appalachia has come about in part because of the region's isolation. Up until the last few decades, there weren't many passable roads. The coal trains chugged in to collect the region's mineral wealth and haul it away. And there's not much flat land to build on. People live stacked up in narrow valleys between mountains — "hollers." You can't build a manufacturing plant in a holler. You can't go into large-scale farming, either. There's no room.

So the fortunes of eastern Kentuckians have largely depended on the economic health and the policies of the coal industry. Too often, hopes pinned on coal have shattered, leaving desolation in their place.

Today the United States doesn't need much coal. What little mining that remains is largely done by machines. Coal mines have laid off thousands of workers over the last decade. There are fewer mining jobs than ever, and there's no reason to believe this is going to change.

Poverty and hardship have a way of grinding people down over a period of time, and the isolation of the mountains makes things even worse. A poor family high up in a holler might have no contact with the rest of the world for weeks or even months. People struggle to survive, to keep the cracks in the house walls patched with old pieces of cardboard, to grow a few vegetables in the summer and to get by on dried beans and corn meal in the winter.

Somehow, most of them still have a glimmer of

hope in their eye. They have a determination to carry on that humbles me.

Most of the mountain people don't want to leave their beautiful region. It's the only home they've ever known, and they love it. To a 75-year-old lady who has seen many sadnesses and many disasters, a mere flood surely is not reason enough to pick up and leave — especially when she knows that God is still here.

"I now set my bow in the clouds and it will be the sign of the covenant between me and the earth," God told Noah once the furious waters had receded.

I looked at the courageous old lady. I looked at the debris that had been her life's possessions. I looked at the mud caking the front step, and the creek rolling by, still angry.

"We still have God," Sadie said. "Remember, He doesn't wash away."

Families

Remember always to welcome strangers, for by doing this, some people have entertained angels without knowing it.

— Hebrews 13:2

When I read those time-honored words of St. Paul, I like to think about the warm hospitality an angel would receive from the mountain folk of eastern Kentucky. Though Appalachian families may not have much, they always want to give you some of what they *do* have. They make you feel like part of the family when you walk through the door.

Joe Foley, CAP's Emergency Assistance Manager in Martin, is out on the road visiting the mountain people every day. He takes distress calls from people in crisis situations, goes to see them to assess their problems first-hand, then arranges whatever help they need. It's a job that's custom-made to produce a high stress level, but Joe says its rewards far outweigh its demands.

"These people have such gratitude and such friendship!" he told me recently. "You're welcomed into the house no matter how poor or how humble.

You're always offered food and coffee. If it's summer, they offer you a cold drink, and when you leave, you're loaded down with vegetables and maybe a quart of pickles or some other treat they've made. The mountain people are very open and very free. The word that comes to mind is 'hospitable.' "

I've received the same gracious welcome many hundreds of times in my years in eastern Kentucky. As Joe says, it is inspiring. The mountain families' gifts of coffee and warm greetings keep our CAP family of staff members and volunteers going strong.

You see, CAP, too, is a family, made up of permanent staff members and as many as 500 volunteers throughout the course of each year. Since our founding, we've benefited from the help of over 35,000 CAP volunteers, a group of people so diverse that I believe only the power of God's love could bind us so closely together. We work together, play together, and pray together, because — though the Christian Appalachian Project does not belong to any one religious denomination — we are Christian, and we try to live as a community in Christ.

Joe Foley has become a member of the CAP family. Just as I believe that God's love has created a family within CAP, I believe God hand-picked Joe Foley to help other families bind themselves together through his Emergency Assistance work.

Emergency Assistance is the first point of contact with CAP for most local people. They come to us when they have no place to live, no food to eat, no money for the utility bills. (Actually, because they are so proud and self-reliant, we often go to them, referred by a concerned friend or relative.)

In other words, Emergency Assistance is the front line of CAP's war against human misery and suffering. And Joe Foley's down-to-earth compassion makes him an ideal Emergency Assistance Manager.

I asked Joe recently if the stress of this position was getting to him. After all, listening to as many as 15 calls for help each day — and knowing that it's your responsibility to do something about them, with limited resources and a very crowded schedule — could be pretty discouraging.

But Joe smiled. "Father," he said, "these people give back what they receive many times over. And it's hard to feel stressed-out yourself when you're dealing with a family that can't afford glasses for the kids and false teeth for the parents! Their problems help me put my life in perspective."

Often, the people do pay us back. As one man said, "Taking a hand-out, it makes you feel lower than a snake's belly." Sometimes those who receive Emergency Assistance funds decide to give as much back as possible when their situations improve, so we can help their neighbors. These families might give just a few dollars a month in contributions to CAP, but their gifts are especially meaningful to us, because they tell us that the folks we've helped are managing on their own again. CAP beneficiaries help us out in other ways, too, contributing their special skills and time as volunteers.

That's the way the mountain people want it. They don't want hand-outs. That's why it's so rewarding to lend them a helping hand, because you know that's all they need to get proudly back on their feet again.

Take the case of Becky and John, for example. Like many other poor families, they lived in a trailer in one of the hollers. One cold night, the trailer went up in flames. Thank God, Becky and John and their three little ones escaped unharmed. But everything they owned was destroyed.

Burn-outs like this one happen too often in Appalachia, where families try desperately to keep warm by burning cheap kerosene or oil heaters, or by burning coal or wood in stoves that aren't safe. The charred remains of too many houses and trailers scar the landscape here, depressing reminders of lives and homes lost.

A burn-out is just one of the calamities that can bring a proud mountain family to its knees. Disaster comes in many forms: Floods. Losing a job. Death or serious illness. A landlord's decision to sell a piece of property.

Sadly, tragedies like burn-outs are almost routine here. But that doesn't mean there's anything routine about Joe's Emergency Assistance work.

"Each family has special needs," Joe explains. "And it's often a challenge to meet those needs, because Emergency Assistance can only do so much. We do run out of resources, and that's when my job is the hardest. I hate to have to turn people away when they're in a tough spot.''

Usually, Joe doesn't have to say ''no'' to those in real need. He can tap into the CAP network to meet the particular needs of a family. The Christian Appalachian Project is actually a coalition of many different programs. We've grown by adding on a new arm or leg whenever we saw a need to be met. CAP's not a massive bureaucracy, but a big family of different programs interweaving to serve eastern Kentucky's people however we can.

So if a burned-out family needs clothes, Joe can send them to one of our Attic Stores, where good-quality used clothing can be selected at low or no cost. If the wind is blowing through cracks in the walls, we send our Home Repair crew to help patch the place together. If a family has no home at all, we can usually find them temporary housing. If they need food, we get them to one of the area's food pantries. If they need medical care, we take them to the doctor and make sure the bills are covered. If they need counseling, we refer them to our Family Life Center. And so on.

We draw on all of CAP's resources to get a family back on its feet again after disaster strikes. Then we help them help themselves, working with them as they make long-term improvements in their situation — changes that we hope will free them from the degradation of poverty.

A young mother named Mag recently thanked

me for what CAP had done for her family. Her husband had lost his job. (That's not uncommon here. The unemployment rate is three times the national average!) The couple and their two little ones had nothing to live on once the unemployment ran out. Relatives, themselves in tight circumstances, could only help so much.

One winter day, Mag and her husband had no oil left to heat the house, and the electric company was threatening to cut off their lights. Without an emergency loan, the family would be plunged into cold and darkness.

I asked Mag what she did after she received the utility company's cut-off notice.

"I'll tell you what I did," she said, her bright blue eyes filming over with tears. "I just laid down and cried!"

Mag's not the type to give up, even momentarily. She is hard-working and resourceful. In fact, last summer she received some seeds and canning jars through CAP's Small Farm program, and she grew and canned 400 quarts of vegetables for her family!

But hard times can knock even the strongest woman off her feet. Mag didn't know where to turn. And if she'd had a choice, she would have solved her problem on her own. When you're proud, you don't want to go to strangers for help.

But when you see your children suffering, you swallow your pride.

I'm glad that Mag heard about CAP. We were

able to work out an arrangement with the electric company to keep her lights on, and we got her some oil to heat her house.

Mag has more than repaid us with many hours of cheerfully given service to CAP. It has been a pleasure and a privilege for our CAP staff to get to know her and her family better. We've also been able to extend a bit more help. Mag's youngest son was 5 years old when we got to know him. He was having trouble in kindergarten — "flunking," as Mag said.

It's no wonder the little boy had troubles. There was no money to get him good, warm clothing. There was no money for school supplies. And the meals Mag could afford to feed her little ones were not always adequate.

With CAP's help and his parents' continuing guidance, the boy is doing much better now. He has clothes and books and pencils and tablets, and three good square meals a day. And he's making straight A's in first grade!

I wish you could meet this bright little boy. Like many of the mountain children, he has blond hair and bright blue eyes. One day I asked him about his mother's garden, and he told me proudly, "I like beans, and spinach, and taters!" He is open, affectionate, and well-behaved because of the good upbringing his mother and father have given him. In spite of all their troubles, Mag and her husband have been good parents. It has broken their hearts not to be able to give their children more.

"There's nothing a kid likes better than a book," Mag told me. "You know, a kid'll get himself a book and get wrapped up in it and just be as happy as can be! But lots of times, folks around here can't buy their kids books. My little ones love the books CAP gave us."

I hope Mag is right. I hope the mountain children really do like nothing better than books. They will need to love books and writing and arithmetic to break the chain of poverty. They need, above all else, education — something their parents often did not get.

But it's never too late to learn. That's why we have developed our GED and Adult Literacy Programs. We want to help people get the schooling they need to get better employment, to teach their own kids to read and love learning — and to gain the dignity and self-esteem that come with the ability to read.

According to the 1980 Census, we've got a long way to go. Kentucky's Fifth Congressional District, where most of our programs are located, has the highest percentage of adults without high school diplomas of any district in the nation.

Worse yet, in some parts of eastern Kentucky, one out of every three adults is illiterate!

It's easy to take reading for granted. I know I do. I've been reading all my life, in order to learn, to grow, to know more about the Lord and His world.

I can't imagine not being able to read.

But if you can't read, there are so many other things you can't do. Here's a list of just a few of those "impossible" tasks:

- *reading a road sign.* That means travelling to a new place is very difficult. Try to imagine driving to an unknown location when you can't read a highway or street sign!

Illiteracy can mean that a man or woman will not be able to go apply for a job, or take a sick child to a medical specialist.

- *filling out forms.* If you can't read, it's tough even to get a driver's license. Applying for a lease on an apartment, opening a bank account, filling out a job application — these tasks can be insurmountable.

- *educating your children.* What if you couldn't read your child a story at bedtime? That's bad enough. But it's just the beginning of the things illiterate parents cannot do for their children.

They can't help with homework. They can't write a note to the teacher or read the kids' report cards. They can't teach them the joy of reading — a joy that truly changes and enriches lives.

Some illiterate parents are so ashamed of their own shortcomings that they tell their kids school isn't important. "I didn't go to school, and I'm doing okay!" They adopt this defiant attitude to salvage their pride. I understand that. But it frightens me, because it means the next generation of kids will do poorly in school, drop out early, and follow in their parents' footsteps to lead a life of poverty.

- *learning new skills in order to get a job* — or a better job than the one you already have.

David, one of 40 literacy students in CAP's 1988 adult education program in Floyd County, comes from a tiny town called Wayland. He decided to turn his life around by learning to read.

"A lot of guys up there around Wayland, they don't know how — they just laugh at you because you're trying to learn to read. But now I can at least get something out of the newspaper. I used to need a lot of help with these welding books," he said, pointing to the vocational texts on the table in front of him. "Most of it I can do by myself now. Even going to the store is easier because I can read what I buy!"

Because he had the courage to learn to read, David can now move ahead with his welding training, acquiring a valuable skill. He can get past the poverty that ensnares many of his friends in Wayland. And when he becomes a parent, you can bet he'll make sure that his children learn to read and do well in school!

Sister Mary Gervase Lochotzki began CAP's adult education program in eastern Kentucky five years ago. She directs the learn-to-read program and the GED program, which allows adults to finish high school at any age by studying at their own pace for a General Equivalency Diploma.

Sister Gervase says that many of the mountain folk want to learn to read so they can read the Bible. "Some are interested in helping their children read. Some come because of their jobs. Others want to read because basically they are tired of living in fear that somebody is going to ask them to read something that they can't. So many people have been taken advantage of because they can't read."

Donna Yellen, formerly manager of CAP's Emergency Assistance Program in Floyd County, volunteered as a literacy tutor. "I realized after I started tutoring that reading is by far the most valuable gift I could give anybody. Out of all the things I did in my years in Appalachia" — and Donna has done plenty — "I feel like this is the most important."

Knowing how to read is a cornerstone to feeling good about yourself. It's a key to good citizenship, effective parenting, self-reliance, freedom, and personal dignity. I'm very proud of what Sister Gervase accomplishes with her adult education programs. In 1987 alone, 112 literacy tutors were trained and 136 new students entered the GED program. At any given time, 30 to 40 students are being taught to read. That adds up to hundreds of people a year changing their lives profoundly through education — taking the first important step toward breaking the grip of poverty on their lives and the lives of their families.

Of course, changes like these don't happen overnight. It takes time to learn to read. It takes time and energy and courage to change your life for the better.

And it takes time and energy and God's love to help a family grow into a strong and nurturing place for all its members — a place where an angel who happens by will be pleased, not only by the warm welcome he receives, but also by the caring he sees between his mortal cousins.

Our CAP family is here to foster that love. We pray that we will know the true meaning of hospitality. And we try to learn it in the lessons the mountain people teach us every day.

A Haven and a Refuge

*God himself has said: I shall not fail or desert
you, and so we can say with confidence: With
the Lord on my side, I fear nothing: what can
human beings do to me?*
— Hebrews 13:5-6

"I don't tell my mother what I do at CAP,"
Regina Collins told me.

She was kidding — sort of. Regina works at one
of our Spouse and Child Abuse Shelters. Her mother
knows that. But Regina doesn't bother her mother
with some of the details — like the courage it takes
to accompany an abused wife to court when her
estranged husband might very possibly show up with
a shotgun.

"I had no idea what I was getting into when I
started working at the shelter," Regina admitted. This
talented young registered nurse started at CAP as
a volunteer in Preventive Health. Like so many other
CAP volunteers, she fell in love with eastern Kentucky and decided to stay on. That's lucky for the
women and children who seek refuge from violent
homes, because Regina is one of those rare human

beings who is willing to put her own life on the line to help others.

And we need all the Reginas we can find, because spouse abuse is often a life-or-death matter in eastern Kentucky. It's hard to understand why a man — or a woman — would knowingly be cruel to the people he or she loves most. Why does the family — the center of love for children and adults alike — become a battle ground?

I'm not an expert on spouse and child abuse. But I do know that poverty and unemployment and despair can build up in an otherwise loving man until his only outlet is a torrent of angry words, a hard slap across a tender face.

At CAP, we try to help the offenders as well as the victims. To my way of looking at it, family violence in Appalachia is one more tragic symptom of poverty's destructive force. But our first concern is to provide a refuge for women who have decided to flee a violent situation. Our Spouse and Child Abuse Centers give frightened, battered wives and children safe harbor in the midst of terrible storms in their lives.

With the help of God and our community, the centers have brought healing into the lives of abuse victims. But it's not an easy process.

If you haven't experienced family violence, it's hard to imagine its profound effects. Take the case of Joshua, for example. This beautiful little four-year-old came to the shelter with his two-year-old sister and their mom, who had been battered as long as the little boy could remember.

Joshua was unruly. None of our child therapist's usual techniques calmed him. Joshua's behavior went far beyond most childlike mischief. He would hit, bite, and kick his mother repeatedly, leaving scars and bruises.

Once she had built a rapport with Joshua, CAP's child therapist asked the little boy, "Why do you beat Mommy up?"

"I have to," Joshua said. "Daddy's not here to love Mommy any more, so I have to do it."

For Joshua, kicking, biting, and hitting equalled loving. That was all he had ever known from his father. He was simply trying to be the man of the house, to fill his father's shoes.

What a sad conclusion for this little boy to reach! Joshua's story is a heart-breaking example of what happens in families plagued by violence. There are many Joshuas in these mountains. Sadder still, there are too many women like Annie.

When Regina tries to tell Annie's story, her eyes fill with tears. "All the staff was close to her," she said. "She had such a bright outlook. She always had a smile for everyone. And her little two-year-old was so adorable."

Annie was in her early twenties when she came to the shelter to escape a violent husband. After a time, she got stronger and moved out to live with her grandmother and re-build her life and the life of her child. The CAP shelter staff thought she was doing well. But then they received devastating news: Annie was dead.

She had gone back to live with her husband. "I guess she just couldn't believe he would ever really do this to her," Regina told me. Annie had been asleep in bed. Her husband woke her up, yelling angrily at her about something. Then he shot her with a high-powered handgun.

At least he did not kill their child.

I know it is hard for the CAP shelter staffers and volunteers to carry on after losing one of "their" ladies. But they must. So many more Annies would die without their help. So many more children would never have a chance to grow up whole and healthy.

"I believe that one person can be a kid's savior," Regina said. "Because this kid can see in you that life can be better, that not all adults fight — this child might make it. That pulls me through. I know I can make a difference."

Success stories from the shelters are a real testament to the human spirit. There's a wonderful lady named Helena whose story is especially inspiring. Helena came to the shelter after 35 years of marriage to a disturbed and violent man. She had suffered intolerable degradation at the hands of her husband, who kept a machete under the mattress of their bed and told her repeatedly that one day she wouldn't wake up.

Helena's husband wouldn't let her handle money,

and he didn't want to pay the heating bills. So Helena chopped wood to burn in the stove. Even so, her husband wouldn't let her sit in the same room with him, so she couldn't sit next to the stove to keep warm in winter. He wouldn't let her go to the doctor, though she has been a diabetic for many years. (Her eyes sustained damage that could have been prevented had she received good medical care.) He shot at her. He terrorized her.

After 35 years, you would think Helena wouldn't have the courage to get up and walk out. But she did. And today she is a new person. She spent a good deal of time at the shelter at first, where the staff admits to having babied her. Now she lives in an apartment of her own. Impeccably dressed and groomed, Helena is an attractive, vital woman who comes to the shelter often to visit with her new friends.

Helena needed love. She needed to be told, over and over again, that she deserved respect and freedom as a person. She needed medical care and help finding a place to live, assistance in filing for divorce and instruction in how to handle her finances. Because of the generosity of donors all across America, and because of the hard work of our shelter staffers, CAP was able to give Helena what she needed — what she so truly deserved after decades of torment.

We also see wonderful transformations in the children who come with their mothers to our shelter. They too receive medical care and counseling and support to put their little lives back together. Often, they have been pushed to one side while their parents struggled violently with one another. We try to give them their childhood back, and it's wonderful when we succeed, as we did with little Lisa.

This blonde-haired, blue-eyed toddler had been neglected and sexually abused. When she came to the shelter, she wouldn't talk to anybody. Understandably, she didn't trust anyone. Our child therapist worked long and hard to show Lisa that somebody did care. And her love turned Lisa around.

Today Lisa babbles on excitedly, as you'd expect a healthy toddler to do. She's doing well in nursery school. She loves her special little white patent leather purse with lace on it and her matching shoes.

Lisa is a happy little girl today. Helena is learning to live again. There are hundreds more who come to us each year, fleeing a vicious anger they cannot understand. We help as much as we can, as much as they will let us.

And we wonder how many more women and children are living in fear in these hollers — how many more need us but are too afraid to try to break away. We can only pray that they will find the courage they need to change their lives, and that we will have the grace to know how to help them when they do.

The Children of the Mountains

"Little ones to Him belong,
They are weak but He is strong."

It was Easter, some 15 years ago. I had already
served quite a few years in eastern Kentucky, but I
guess you could say I wasn't shock-proofed yet. (I'm
not sure I ever will be.)

Accompanied by some volunteers from out of
state, I was visiting local families. One of the families
lived in a little shack along a creek. I had met this
family at Christmastime while checking on people
who might need help with food, clothing, and toys.
Now, a few months later, I led the volunteers down
a mud path and across the little creek. We knocked
on the door and told the husband who we were. He
ushered us into the gloom of the cabin. A dim glow
flickered from the open fireplace, the family's only
source of heat.

We met his wife and talked for a little while. She
mentioned her baby. I asked if I might see the child.
The husband and wife took us over to a little place
in the corner of the room. There, in the dark, lay

their two-month-old child — not in a crib or a bassinet, a cradle or even a pillow-lined basket. This child, the family's most precious treasure, lay in a cage made of tightly woven chicken wire.

After a moment of stunned silence, my curiosity and concern got the better of me, and I asked the parents why they had their little child in this cage. I'll never forget the answer:

"We have to have him in this little cage, so that the rats won't eat on him."

It wasn't cruelty that motivated this father when he took the chicken wire and built the cage. On the contrary. Like nearly every parent, he deeply loved his newborn son. No doubt he built the cage with love in his hands and desperation in his heart.

I guess many people wouldn't believe this story. Most people don't think that such a thing could happen in the America we know. But in a little shed along a creek in Appalachian country, it was reality.

You might think things have improved enough so that no child could possibly be living in such circumstances. After all, the 21st century is fast approaching. Our American standard of living has never been higher.

But that great standard of living has not found its way to many people in Appalachia. Children still live in dire poverty, growing up on a daily diet of despair and deprivation.

Perhaps more than anything else, that's the thing I most want to change in Appalachia. I want to see the children — our future — healthy, happy, and able to break the cycle of poverty they are born into.

And that's one reason why we of the Christian Appalachian Project focus much of our energy and resources on the children.

The other reason? It's simple. We love these kids. You can't help but love them. Maybe I'm prejudiced, but the children of these mountains have always seemed special to me. They are bright and loving, open-hearted and beautiful.

They are eager to learn and to love. Too often, they don't get much of an opportunity.

Take the Johnsons, for just one of many examples. These three little boys — ages 6, 8, and 11 — have had lives harder than most of us will ever have to face.

When a CAP worker visited their home not too long ago, the boys' living conditions made her ill. The filthy old trailer that served as their home could not have been dirtier, inside or out. There was no food in the house.

The boys' mother had died a few years before. Now the boys depended solely upon their father for all the care they received, which wasn't much.

Unfortunately, their father is a hopeless alcoholic. And it is very clear that he grossly neglected the boys after their mother died.

The boys didn't know how to bathe or brush their teeth, so they were as filthy as their surroundings. They had to fend for themselves food-wise. The eldest would take whatever money his dad gave him and go to the store. Being all of 11 years old, he bought junk food for himself and his brothers. They lived mostly on candy bars and soda pop and chips, when they had anything to eat at all. Sometimes they would try to cook something for themselves. The 6-year-old burned himself badly trying to fix his own breakfast just last year.

The boys are painfully thin. Malnutrition has stunted their growth. But their potential has not been stunted — not by the loss of their mother, not by the abject poverty surrounding them, not by the terrible burden of living with a severely addicted father.

You can imagine that our CAP workers wanted to do everything possible for these boys. They talked the father into letting CAP take care of the children for a while. We arranged for counseling and rehabilitation for the father, hoping that one day he will be able to take care of his children. We gave the children the basics all children should have: a decent home, loving and responsible adults to care for them, running water, soap, toothpaste, three nutritious meals a day, and medical care. To the Johnson boys, these basics were luxuries. And they bloomed under our care.

Can you imagine the joy the two younger boys felt when they attended CAP's summer camp? They had never had toys. They had hardly gone to school at all, so even a playground would be a big thrill for them. Now here they were in a beautiful environment, with so many other children to play with, a lake to swim in, games and sports to enjoy. It must have seemed like heaven to them!

One of the camp counselors told me about a conversation he overheard between the Johnson boys at camp:

"This sure is fun, isn't it?" the eight-year-old said to his little brother.

"Yeah!"

"I sure do miss Mommy, don't you?"

"I sure do."

We can never heal their heartbreak entirely. But we can try, and we do try, every day.

CAP's programs for children run the gamut, from six Child Development Centers for the littlest ones to Mountain Christian Academy, a private school where at least some of the mountain children can get a high-quality elementary and junior high education.

We provide day care with love and lots of education at our Child Development Centers. Unless they can enroll their children in these CAP programs, many parents cannot get or keep a job. CAP wants to make it possible for parents to work, knowing their children are being well cared for, so that fewer families will depend on public assistance. The CAP Child Development Centers do a beautiful job of easing parents' minds and giving youngsters a head start with high-quality educational programs.

For children with special needs, CAP sponsors

Parents Are Teachers and several residential homes. Through Parents Are Teachers, families with pre-school-age handicapped children learn to help their special children reach their potential with educational activities and physical therapy.

Sometimes, though, these children cannot stay with their families. That's where CAP's Special Needs Home and Rainbow Respite Care Center come into play.

Pat Montgomery manages CAP's Rainbow Respite Care Center, where handicapped children and adults stay for brief periods while their families take much-needed breaks from caring for them. The Respite Center boasts many wonderful activities for its guests: bowling, canoeing, picnics, crafts — things handicapped people may never have experienced before. The Respite Center also works with its guests to develop independent living skills.

But the most important thing about the Rainbow Respite Care Center is that it gives families a chance to rest, knowing that their handicapped loved ones are in good hands. When a family chooses to take care of a quadriplegic, or a severely mentally retarded child, they have made a total commitment that often makes it impossible for them to do things most people take for granted — like going out to dinner, or on vacation.

Pat Montgomery remembers one lady in particular, who hadn't had a break from taking care of her 12-year-old, totally paralyzed son for six years.

"She hadn't been able to go see her other kids play sports at school. She hadn't been able even to go to the grocery store! She told me she was just about at the end of her rope when she got a letter from us announcing that the Rainbow Respite Care Center had opened. It was truly an answer to her prayers. She and her husband took a week-long vacation while we cared for her son. I'm sure that break gave her the energy to keep on going."

It's hard to imagine how important that respite might be — not just for the mother and her paralyzed son, but also for the other children in the family, who had felt neglected for so many years because their brother commanded the attention of his parents nearly all the time.

It's great to know you're helping a family stay together — or that you're creating a family where there has never been one before. At the Special Needs Home, CAP's Gloria Jordan tries to provide a real family for emotionally and physically handicapped children who quickly accept each other's handicaps and think of each other as brothers and sisters.

The kids really care about one another. One small boy who is confined to a wheelchair at the Special Needs Home receives extra doses of love from his housemates. "Few of the kids walk by him without patting his head, kissing him, or straightening his blanket," Gloria says.

While the handicapped children have problems that require a lot of special attention, some of Appalachia's little ones have been in danger of death because they lacked something very simple to provide — like transportation. We don't often think of owning a car as a dire necessity. But one local family could have lost their little daughter unless someone stepped in to help.

An adorable two-year-old, Misty Lee, has leukemia. When the diagnosis was made, her father was out of work. The family was living in a modest little house, barely getting by. Now, to save their daughter's life, they would have to drive to Lexington, two and a half hours away, to the University of Kentucky Medical Center, every two weeks, sometimes more often.

At first, the family rented a car. But it cost them between $100 and $125 to make the trip. Although the American Cancer Society eventually helped them with a five-cents-per-mile travel reimbursement, they simply could not afford the repeated trips. In desperation, Misty Lee's mother got in touch with CAP.

All of us at CAP wanted badly to help little Misty Lee. So did the rest of the community. Mike Sanders, director of CAP's Martin, Kentucky operations, asked singer Marlow Tackett to perform a benefit concert for Misty at Mountain Christian Academy. A crowd turned out to sing and dance and raise money for Misty Lee. Local businesses gave donations to have their advertisements put in the concert flyer. Martin's Youth Center teenagers put on a "Bike-a-Thon" for Misty Lee. All in all, the community raised over $1,000 for the little girl and her family.

Fortunately, while looking for a car, I received a special donation for Misty Lee's family — a good quality automobile. Now they could keep the $1,000 as their emergency fund. They wouldn't have to put it into an old jalopy to get them from Floyd County to Lexington.

When Mike Sanders called Misty Lee's dad to tell him that he could keep the extra money, the man was astonished. "I wanted to let CAP take the money they raised and give it to other people who needed it, because all we really needed was the car, that's all we could ask for, but Mr. Sanders, well, he said that all that money was ours."

Misty Lee is doing fine now. Her dad is working at the Floyd County Health Department. The family has a car and some emergency money to fall back on. And we can thank the Lord for the continued health of one beautiful little girl and the love a whole community showed when she needed help.

I'm proud of the local people who helped a little girl in need. Of course, for most people, it's easy to help children, because they give you back so much love and joy. They make you laugh. They lighten your heart. The good Lord knows my heart has needed lightening at times over the years. The little ones of eastern Kentucky have provided me with many merry moments.

Take the preschoolers at CAP's Sunshine Center.

These three- to five-year-olds were learning to do a
little cooking, and their teacher collected their recipes
for a special cookbook called *Nutrition with Love:
Children's Recipes (and Other Stuff)*. It's a cookbook
classic, containing gourmet recipes like these:

APPLESAUCE
3 pears

Cook pears in pan at low temperature for one minute.
Eat hot.

CORN
5 corns
5 glasses water

Cook all day on low temperature. Eat.

FISH
Ketchup   Fish Skin
Chicken   Bread Crumbs
Fish

Put fish in a big deep pan. Put fish skin on the fish
and put chicken inside it. Put pan in oven at 142
degrees for two minutes. Take out of oven. Put on
plate. Put ketchup on the skin and eat it.

Here's a recipe even I can manage:

CEREAL
Put milk on it.

A child also gave me one of my favorite and funniest memories of my years in Appalachia. I was preaching in a small mission church in Mount Vernon, Kentucky. We had such a tiny congregation that we asked a five-year-old boy to take up the collection. He eagerly agreed, and, even at his tender age, he understood that we needed to collect as much money as possible.

The young man shouldered his duty admirably. But after passing the collection basket in front of a visitor to the church, he stopped still, refusing to budge. His mother leaned across several pews to get his attention. "Frank! Go on! Go on to the next place!" The little boy stood stock-still.

Again his mother urged him to move along. Frank had other ideas. "But mother, he didn't put in hardly anything at all!" Frank called back to his mother in a loud, piping voice.

Needless to say, the visitor was out the door long before the rest of us.

The children have given me great joy. Over the years, I have tried to give them some of the childhood pleasures they have been missing. CAP's summer camps are a big part of this effort. So many of these kids have never known what it's like to be carefree, to play games, to laugh in the bright mountain sunshine, or to enjoy something as simple as a rowboat ride. Our camps give them these delights each summer for a week or so. The camp experience shows the kids that there's a lot to look forward to in life

— more than they might have known about before.

At camp, they also learn that there are adults they can confide in, adults who care. I'll never forget a young boy who came to our camp from a troubled family. He came and sat next to me by the campfire on his first night.

"You found out about the stealing, didn't you?" he asked.

I said, "No, I don't know anything about the stealing. But I'd like to help you if there's anything I can do."

The boy sighed. He told me how he had stolen a bicycle from one of the neighborhood children.

"Why did you take the bicycle?" I asked him.

"I wanted to be like everyone else," he told me. "Everyone I knew had something to play with, something to have fun with. At our house we didn't have anything. I wanted to be like everybody else, so I took the bicycle. They had three of them at their house and we didn't have any."

Of course the child was wrong to steal the bicycle. But why shouldn't he want to be like everyone else? Why shouldn't he share the normal desires of every child? There ought to be a way that all poor children can know the joy and fun of playing and laughing. Too many of our mountain children are sad. They don't know what it is to laugh. They don't know how to play.

I remember a young girl in a family that was very poor. Her mother was extremely ill and paralyzed. Everything had to be done for her: change her clothes, feed her, wash her, take care of her every need. The family's eldest child was an 11-year-old girl. It fell upon her to cook the meals, to care for the mother, to do all the things around the house that needed doing, and to look after her four younger brothers and sisters. The father did what he could to go out and rake up enough for them to eat.

The little girl was forced to act like a woman. For a while, she handled her enormous burdens. Then one day, the father came home and found the little girl holding a pillow firmly over her mother's face.

The little girl had snapped. She could take no more. All she knew was that somehow she had to have some relief. Her mother was the biggest problem, and so she tried to suffocate her. The father came just in time to save the mother's life.

Like the little girl, I am only human. At times, I'm tempted to give up, to say "What's the use? It's too much work. The problems can't be solved. I can't do any more." I get tired of begging people for the money we need to care for Appalachia's children, its needy, its elderly.

But when I'm at my most discouraged, I remember the boy who stole a bicycle in a pitiful attempt to be like everybody else. I remember the girl who tried to end her mother's life with a pillow so she could have a little rest. And I know that I must go on. It is up to us big people to help the little people make their way in the world. Without our caring, they don't have a chance.

Our Lord Jesus loved children with a special tenderness. He rebuked His disciples when they tried to keep the little ones away from Him. "Let the little children come to Me," He said. He told us we can only enter His Kingdom with childlike hearts.

The Lord calls us to care for the children just as He does. It is a privilege and a joy to be able to answer His call.

A Bountiful Harvest

From the soil, Yahweh God caused to grow every kind of tree, enticing to look at and good to eat.

— Genesis 2:9

"If I'm nervous or upset about something, I just get out and work in the garden, and it relaxes me," Ann said. "It's a way to get close to the Lord."

Ann lives in Garrard County, Kentucky. She and her three young children don't have a lot of money. But, through Ann's work in the garden, they have wonderful fresh food throughout the growing season and jar after jar of canned vegetables put away for the long, dreary winter.

Ann participates in CAP's Small Farms Program. Each year, her family is one of over one thousand area households to receive free seed potatoes, vegetable and flower seeds, fertilizer, pesticide, canning jars, and other assistance. CAP receives many of the materials for Small Farms from corporate donors all over America. Their generosity really makes a mark on the Appalachian landscape once spring and summer roll around.

Gardeners like Ann can't afford to buy seed, fertilizer, or canning jars for themselves. Small Farms not only gives them the necessities for growing a garden — it gives them the incentive. And food is just the start of what gardening gives Ann and her children.

"Once you've gardened, it becomes a part of you," says Keith Gilbertson, manager of the Small Farms Program in the western part of CAP's service area. "There are intangible benefits. People maintain pride. They feel like they're doing something. For a lot of the people we serve, the garden keeps them going. It's something to hope for, to look forward to."

What do the mountain folk like to grow? You name it. Their carefully tended gardens boast bumper crops of beans, corn, beets, cucumbers, tomatoes, onions, mustard greens, pumpkins, potatoes, peas, carrots, lettuce, squash, spinach, turnips, and radishes. Some dedicated gardeners request okra, cabbage, and other special seeds, and we do our best to get them. We always try to throw in at least one packet of flower seeds per family, to encourage gardeners to beautify their homes.

The Small Farms Program is one way to plant pride and self-reliance in Appalachia. Beyond simply helping people supplement their food budget, Small Farms gives them something constructive and creative to do for themselves. It brings families together and gives them a feeling of accomplishment — something that is sorely needed by the unemployed, by those who are partially disabled or ill, by the isolated elderly.

I understand how the Small Farm participants feel about their gardens. There's nothing that lifts the spirits more than the wonder of tender green plants breaking up through the soil, the smell of ripe tomatoes basking in the hot summer sun, the pleasure of picking fresh sweet corn off the stalk and running into the house to cook it and enjoy its incomparable flavor.

I'd love to put in a big vegetable plot each year myself, but I don't have time. I have to be content with the porch on my house in Martin, where I keep quite a collection of houseplants. To see them growing and thriving brings me great joy. It gives me the feeling that I have accomplished something wonderful — though of course I know that I'm just helping God's system along when I care for the plants.

I also understand our eastern Kentucky gardeners who often say that they feel closest to God when they're working in the garden. CAP workers try to enhance that feeling by sharing friendship throughout the growing season with the Small Farmers. "Just being that Christian witness and friend in that home has a lot of influence on people's lives," Keith Gilbertson says.

Joe Foley, CAP's Emergency Assistance Manager in Martin, feels that the Small Farms Program is one of CAP's most rewarding efforts. "We visit throughout the spring and summer, and the people get a chance to give to us, not the other way around. The Small Farms Program is based on real friendship. You can never leave a family in the summer without an armload of their vegetables. This is their chance to show off. It's their way of giving back and not feeling beholden to CAP. We don't want to destroy their pride and initiative — just the opposite. So the Small Farms Program is really something special."

CAP gives away somewhere between 30,000 and 35,000 seed packets each spring. Since we buy or receive donations of seed in large bulk quantities, it's an enormous task to divide up the seed, put it in smaller seed envelopes, and label the packets. The whole CAP family gets into the action, from volunteers visiting from out of state, to handicapped workers at our CAPrice sheltered workshop, to area families who are eager to do something to help CAP. It's hard to estimate just how many hours go into preparing the seed and other items for Small Farms distribution. But whatever it takes, it's worth it.

CAP believes in people doing for themselves. And so do the people we serve. They're not looking for handouts. They want to take care of themselves. The Small Farms Program is one of the best examples of this positive, self-sufficient attitude. Garden by garden, person by person, season by season — eventually eastern Kentuckians will find a way to rebuild their beloved Appalachia.

I hope CAP can continue to be a part of their growing process, from seed-time to rich, fulfilling harvest.

The Elders

Now that I am old and grey-haired, God, do not desert me.

— Psalm 71:18

Above all else, Elsie hated the snakes.

Now that she was living in a 10' x 12' abandoned chicken coop, it was hard to keep away from them. Black snakes and garter snakes, she knew, could not kill her; still, it frightened her to think of them crawling over her in the night.

And Elsie knew that the hills were home to deadly snakes as well — copperheads and rattlesnakes.

She put pieces of cardboard boxes against the crumbling floor boards and walls to try to keep them out. Meanwhile, the rain would drum in through nail-holes in the tin roof. All her worldly belongings were piled on the narrow iron bed to keep the snakes and rats out of them. There wasn't much room left for Elsie to sit down or sleep.

When she needed water, Elsie had to walk a quarter of a mile to draw up a bucket of water from a neighbor's well. That's a half-mile to get a drink of water and return home.

How did Elsie, who had lived a long and good life in these hard mountains, come to be living in a chicken coop?

Her alcoholic husband threw her out one day. She had nowhere to go. She knew no one who could take her in. She had no money and no way to earn a living. So she found the chicken coop and she took the few things left to her and she moved in.

When I met Elsie, it was October. She was facing the bleak winter without heat or light or running water, without protection of any kind from snow and ice.

I took one look at the place she called home. It was not good enough to dignify with the term "shack." I knew the Christian Appalachian Project had to find Elsie another home, fast.

I just didn't know how we were going to do it.

It would take $1,000 to buy her a used trailer. I had $250 from Project Emergency funds to spend for Elsie's new home. I didn't know where I'd find the rest of the money. But, as so often happens, the Lord's hand intervened.

Someone gave me $1,000 to build a chapel in one of the mountain towns, a chapel to glorify God's son. I thought it over and decided God would be just as pleased if I used this money to take care of His daughter. The donor of the $1,000 agreed. So we bought Elsie a nice used trailer and put it down where water could be hooked up to it.

Now Elsie had to walk just a few steps, instead of a quarter-mile, to get a drink of water. She had a potbelly stove to heat her new home. But she still had no electricity — no refrigerator, no lights.

By Christmas, some friends and I put together the money to have the electricity installed. We agreed among ourselves that we would pay Elsie's electric bills. Now she can have light in the evening-time of winter. She can have a fan in the heat of summer. She can keep milk and meat and not have it spoil.

Elsie's story has a happy ending. I'm grateful for that. But there are many, many others like her in these hollers. So often the elderly live alone, and they come to be neglected as the years pass and family moves away. They are forgotten. Sometimes, as in the case of Cecil, whom I told you about earlier in this book, nobody even knows they are alive.

It seems to me the forgotten elderly could turn to us and rightfully say: "I've lived a long life. I've done much for this land. I've cultivated the sides of the hills, I've cleared the forest, I've raised a family — and now I'm alone and poor."

Many of them probably wonder why they were born, if this is their reward for a long life of struggle. But they don't say that.

They are usually meek and mild, grateful for the little things we do for them, humble and shy.

Their gentleness of spirit inspires all of us at CAP to seek out the lonely elderly, to make sure they have the medical care they need, good food, warm clothes, and a place to live that's warm and equipped with a bathroom and running water. Through our elderly programs, we befriend eastern Kentucky's older folks. We find out what they need, and we try to provide it.

Sometimes they just need a visit every few weeks, or a ride to the doctor now and then. Sometimes they need a whole new home, like Elsie, or like Dennis.

Dennis was over 75 years old when CAP volunteers first got to know him. He was living in a tiny camper trailer parked on land that belonged to a mining company. It was filthy and decrepit. The rain came in and so did the bugs and mice and rats.

Dennis didn't mind the company of the animals. Even though the mice would eat his dry milk out of the box, he didn't begrudge them. "They have to eat too," he says. "Nature, out in the woods, the wild woods, it's the best part of life to me."

Dennis has an uncommon commitment to God's creatures, a bond with them forged over years of living outdoors in the mountains himself. He prefers not to eat meat, subsisting instead mainly on cashews, peanut butter, watermelons, apples, and bananas. Every day he wades into the creek behind his home to feed the opossum that comes to visit. His expert calls draw bird and animal visitors from all around. Dennis nearly cries when he sees that an animal has been killed on the roadside, or, worse yet, deliberately killed by human hands.

"What kind of man would kill a little birdie like a whippoorwill?" Dennis asks sorrowfully. "They used to be so many of them around here, but now they're gone, all gone. They killed them all." He shakes his head. He calls the whippoorwill's lovely call, remembering the days when their song filled the air.

I suspect that if Dennis had his way, he would still live out among the creatures, using his extensive knowledge of the mountains and nature to fend for himself. But age has forced him indoors. Dennis had a stroke a few years back that left him partially paralyzed. He had to go to the hospital, and from there he was sent to a nursing home.

Dennis couldn't stand being boxed in at the nursing home. He got up one day and walked 25 miles back to his place in Price, Kentucky, dragging the paralyzed part of his body slowly along by using a crutch.

When he got there, he found that his little home had burned to the ground.

He lived in a tent for awhile. Then someone gave him a van, which he slept in for a few years. Then he got the camper he was living in when we found him.

The first thing we did was put a tarpaulin over the camper's roof so the rain wouldn't come in. We wanted to do more immediately. But Dennis is an independent man. We knew we couldn't try to make him move anywhere, or do anything he didn't truly want to do.

One day Bill Brunscheen, a CAP volunteer who had befriended Dennis, asked the old man what he would most like God to give him if he could have anything he wanted.

"Would it be too much to ask for running water? I'd love to be able to take a bath," Dennis replied.

These words moved me deeply. Running water — to this poor man it would be an enormous gift, too big even to ask God for without hesitation. I take running water completely for granted. So do most of America's millions of citizens.

Dennis doesn't take anything for granted.

His attitude made it easy for CAP volunteers and staff members to rally around and find a way to give this mountain man a better place to live, with a bathroom, complete with running water, bathtub, sink, and toilet.

Our Home Repair crew did some research and found that it would be less costly to build a little house for Dennis than to repair or replace his trailer. Some long-time friends of CAP in New Jersey raised the money to pay for Dennis's house.

Now the only problem was where to build it, since the mining company told us they would soon be needing the land where Dennis lived. Fortunately, a lady named Gracie Newman generously agreed to let Dennis live on her land in Hi Hat, Kentucky, about two miles up Left Beaver Creek from Price.

"It was in my heart and I wanted to do it, because he was in need," Gracie said. "If you don't help people like Dennis and they're put in front of you, you're going to have to answer for it someday, that's the way I feel about it."

Others in the community did what they could to help give Dennis a home. donating a refrigerator, furniture, and other necessities. The local lumber yard gave CAP a sizable discount on the lumber needed to build his house. Thanks to the local people, to our friends in New Jersey, and to Gracie Newman, today Dennis has a tiny but sturdy new 12' x 33' house complete with living room, bedroom, and bathroom, and little porches on the front and the back.

The CAP folks who had come to know Dennis decided to throw a 79th birthday party for him on a houseboat, inviting other older people in the community. We coaxed the shy Dennis to come, promising good company, birthday cake, and a nice meal.

But when the time came to pick Dennis up, he was gone. Our CAP staff member somehow knew where to look for him. He was hiding down along the railroad tracks behind his house. He had hobbled down the tracks on a pair of crutches to hide, because he was afraid to attend the party.

The CAP staffer convinced Dennis to give the party a try, and he did. He overcame his fear of others long enough to have a good time. At the end of the day, Dennis said, "You know, I reckon that was the best birthday I ever had in my whole life. I guess people aren't so bad after all.''

Today, Judy Crum, CAP's Elderly Program Coordinator in Floyd County, Kentucky, regularly visits Dennis and a host of others. She takes them to the doctor, brings them things they need, and lets them know that there are people in the world who love and care about them. I can't think of anyone better suited to this particular job than Judy. For her, it is totally a labor of love. To see her with the old people is to see God's tender concern in action in an everyday setting.

"I wanted to work at CAP so bad," Judy says. "I grew up right here in Martin. I worked at a bank for a few years and I liked my job. But I just wanted to do more to help people. I kept writing to CAP and calling them until they finally found a job for me. I couldn't be happier. All day, every day, I have the perfect job. I go out and meet wonderful people and I talk with them and pray with them and do little things for them that mean so much."

Judy thanks God for her job at CAP, and we thank God for her. So do the elderly folks she visits, I'm sure — people like Cecil and Dennis and two ladies named Serelda and Lizzie.

Lizzie was helpless, blind and unable to walk more than a few steps without help. Serelda took her in, agreeing to care for her for the rest of her life. They share Serelda's three-room house up in a holler not far from Cecil's place. Together they have made themselves a family, a refuge against the isolation and sorrow of old age in the lonely mountains.

These two ladies remind me of another pair of women I'll never forget, women I met after a long, hard haul up the side of a mountain. Their tiny house perched precariously on the mountainside. I met the ladies, and they told me their story.

The older lady, Jane, owns the little cabin on the mountainside. One day when she was 75 years old, she was out by the tiny dirt road that goes by the front of her house. She saw another older woman walking up the road, toting a bundle, smoking a corn-cob pipe.

The lady with the bundle, Sarah, stopped to talk to Jane. She told her that her brother had thrown her out, and that she had nowhere to go. She was walking down the road, penniless, in her late sixties, with all her possessions on her back. She was looking for a home.

Jane thought for a while. Soon she said, "I don't have much, but if you want to share it with me, you're welcome to."

Jane and Sarah have lived together for five or six years now. They had neither running water nor a bathroom until CAP got them a well and built a little bathroom onto their house. It made such a difference in their lives not to have to go outside to the outhouse! They overwhelmed us with their gratitude.

Jane asked me one day, "How can I thank you?"

My answer came easily. "You already have. You

took Sarah in when she needed you."

How many of us would do the same? Picture this: A stranger walks up to your door without a dollar to her name. You barely have enough to keep yourself alive. Would you — could you — take her in for the rest of her life, no questions asked?

Though I'd like to think that I would answer "yes," I'm not sure I would have. I admire Jane's generosity and her faith. I would say there aren't many people like her, but these mountains are full of stories of compassion and helpfulness and giving. These people don't have much, but they don't hold back on what they do have.

I hope we of the Christian Appalachian Project follow their good examples. "Do not reject me in my old age, nor desert me when my strength is failing," the psalmist prays. I hope CAP does its best to answer that plea with the love the elderly — the living treasures of Appalachia — so truly deserve.

Taking the Show on the Road

Go out to the whole world; proclaim the gospel to all creation.

— Mark 16:15

Since 1951, when I had been in eastern Kentucky for only a short time, I have been trying to obey the Lord's command to preach the Gospel, if not to every creature, at least to as many as I could reach — or to as many as would listen. To do so, I have travelled the twisting, winding back roads of Appalachia each summer, stopping wherever a dozen or more houses sprang up between two mountains, setting up a portable speaker system so as many people as possible could hear the word of the Lord.

Street preaching is one of the main joys of my life as a priest. Through it, the mountain people learn that God is not restricted to the churches — that He is present in the hollers, in a group of laughing children, in their daily lives. I believe street preaching changes people. I wouldn't give it up for the world.

But one thing is certain: In eastern Kentucky, you've got to be willing to sacrifice your dignity if you want to carry the Lord's word into tiny hamlets where prejudice may abound. Especially in the early years of my ministry, when the local people barely had any idea of what a Catholic priest was — and the ideas they did have were definitely unflattering — it was always a little worrisome to come into a new place and start preaching into a microphone.

Thirty-eight years of street preaching has taken me to places with names like Thousand Sticks, Cutshin, Quicksand, and Hell-fer-Sartin (Hell for Certain), Kentucky. (Believe it or not, there are also two towns called Upper Hell-fer-Sartin and Lower Hell-fer-Sartin.) These names bear witness to the difficulties the early pioneers faced as they pressed into the mountains. Most of their descendants carry on a sad tradition of struggling simply to live, in villages and towns and hidden hollers the rest of America has forgotten about. Most of them don't have a church to go to, and many people don't go when they do. Their hard lives have worn them down. They are caught in a web of inertia and depression. Some of them probably believe that God has forgotten them, too.

I want the people of towns like Hell-fer-Sartin to know that they have not been forgotten — not by God, who, the Lord Jesus told us, knows when even one of His little sparrows falls from the air.

So each summer, when the roads are passable after winter ice melts and spring floods recede, I take a crew of volunteers — seminarians and fellow clergymen — in a caravan of cars and a motor home or camper-trailer, and we drive into the remotest valleys. We go to meet the people face to face, to carry God's word to them. I go to show them that they are important to me—that I care enough to go far out of my way, to get tired and dirty, to be inconvenienced for their sakes.

The people repay us with warmth and gratitude and hospitality — most of the time. But it has not always been this way. I'll never forget a trip to one small town in particular. It's hard to forget a place when you come close to meeting your Maker there.

I was there with a priest from Long Island and a group of about a dozen seminarians from all over the country. We were looking forward to preaching that evening on the subject of brotherly love. We quickly found a good place to park, mount our speakers, and plug in our amplifier. Soon our speakers sent the voice of Tennessee Ernie Ford, singing "What a Friend We Have in Jesus," through the community.

A good crowd gathered, eager to hear what we might have to say. In eastern Kentucky, in those days, entertainment was hard to come by. We had the advantage of being a curiosity to people. At least they would come out to see what we were about.

After the seminarians sang a few gospel songs, I started to preach. I talked about why we should love one another. Then I talked about why we should love even those who don't like us. As if on cue, several cars came screeching up. They stopped abruptly along the side of the road, and about a dozen strong, burly young men jumped out of the cars and came running toward the area where I was preaching.

It's fortunate for me that I don't get excited easily. But when the shots started going off above my head, I have to admit I was more than a little concerned.

The young men fired a gun up in the air and threw soda bottles on the cement directly behind me. They succeeded in creating quite a ruckus, but I had the microphone, and I kept preaching. Finally, one of the young men could take no more. He raced up to me and started cursing me.

He made it very clear that he hated me, and why: I was Catholic. I was an outsider. I was intruding on his town. He wanted to punch me in the face.

Since I'd been preaching about loving even those who dislike you, I tried even harder than usual to refrain from anger. I tried to reason with the young man. But soon one of his companions charged up beside him. The second young man, too, had an overwhelming urge to beat me, and my companions, to a pulp.

He grabbed the microphone out of my hand. "We don't need you outsiders," he yelled. He screamed at the crowd, telling them not to listen to us. After two or three minutes of this, I snatched the microphone away from him when he paused to take a breath. I told the crowd I was sorry for the commotion, and resumed my talk about brotherly love.

For a few minutes, all went well. Then suddenly I felt something hit me in the back of my leg. Soon I felt a warmish liquid trickling into my shoe. "I wonder if I've been shot," I thought to myself, but, since it didn't hurt very much, I decided to keep preaching.

I later learned that the missile fired at my leg was just a tomato — a big, ripe, juicy one.

The young men were determined to stop my preaching. Gathering steam, in a drunken haze, they swarmed toward us. I decided I had to protect the seminarians who were with me. I ordered them to get in our cars, roll up the windows, lock the doors, and stay put.

I told the crowd that I could no longer go on talking about brotherly love when people were threatening to kill us and punctuating their threats with gunshots. I told them we were sorry, but that we would have to leave.

I set about taking down our microphones and amplifiers and getting them back into our cars. As I was working, a friend of mine from the area rode up in his pick-up truck. Quickly assessing the situation, he scolded the crowd of young men.

"Don't you know who this is?" he demanded indignantly. "This is Father Beiting from the Christian Appalachian Project. He's done more good for this area than 'most anybody around, and you should be ashamed to treat him this way!"

The young men told this kind gentleman to shut

up and get out of the way before it was too late. Imprudently, he tried to argue with them again.

They unceremoniously picked my friend up, threw him back into his truck, and slammed the door. My one local ally had now been disposed of quite handily.

As I packed up our equipment, the young men continued to shout all kinds of insults and beg me to fight them. I must confess there have been few times in my life when I wanted more to lay aside the Good Book and give them what they wanted: a fight. Of course, they would have outnumbered me by far, but I'm a big man. Inspired by anger, I'm sure I could have had the satisfaction of knocking down at least two or three of them. And believe me, I wanted that satisfaction badly.

Somehow, I avoided that temptation. I was just about done with packing up when I realized I had to retrieve a small suitcase from across the street, right where about six of the hecklers were standing.

I crossed the street and picked up the suitcase. As I did so, one of them gave me a swift, energetic kick. Luckily, it glanced off the side of my leg, but it hit the suitcase, knocking it open. Now I had to pick up its contents, which were spewed all over the sidewalk.

As I started to gather them up, one of the young men came at me, swinging a chain and threatening to hit me in the face with it. By this time, I'd had about as much of this as I cared to take.

"I wish to goodness you would shut up! I am sick and tired of hearing you shout! Now go away!" I said loudly and sternly to the young man.

To my surprise and relief, it worked. He stopped swinging the chain and walked away.

A few minutes later we finally made our exit. As we drove back to our home base 10 miles away in McKee, we were a much more somber group than we had been as we approached the town where we had preached. The priest from Long Island made haste to tell me that he saw no future for himself in street preaching, and that he would do anything possible to support our work, but that he wished to be excused from any further duties on this expedition. I'm sure the seminarians would have made the same request, if they'd had a choice. Fortunately for me, they didn't. They were excellent companions for the rest of the five-week excursion.

I don't blame my colleagues for being discouraged. I was, too. But my discouragement lightened when I ran into my chief heckler just a few weeks later.

I was passing through the town where the trouble had occurred when I stopped at a Dairy Queen for an ice cream cone. There at the counter was one of the ringleaders of the gang of hostile young men. Once he saw me come into the store, he took off, leaving his ice cream on the counter. He flung himself into his car, rolled up the window, and locked the door.

I walked over to his car and said, "Hello, how are you?"

"Oh, okay," he said. He looked nervous.

"Roll down the window so we can talk," I said.

"Oh, no, no, no!" he answered rapidly. "There's no reason to wind down the window. We can talk like we are."

"I haven't seen you since that night a few weeks ago. You look a little different now," I continued. "You seemed a little under the weather then."

"Oh yeah, I feel better now," he hastily assured me.

"Well, tell me when we can do some more talking," I said matter-of-factly.

"No! No! I think we've talked enough," he stammered, turning the key in the ignition. He sped out of the parking lot. I thought to myself how powerful alcohol can be, turning a normal man into a raging would-be prizefighter. I silently wished my friend well, and went in to get my ice cream.

The following summer, with a new crew of seminarians, I returned to the town of the hecklers to preach again. We selected a spot on the road next to a little two-room shed made completely of tin. The widow lady who lived there generously offered us electricity to plug in our amplifiers. A nice crowd gathered and listened to our singing and preaching.

When we were done, the widow lady came up to me and said, "I wish that you would take this." She pressed a five-dollar bill into my hand.

I told her she had done quite enough for us by letting us use her electricity. I could see that five dollars was an awful lot of money to her, and that she needed it much more than we did.

But she insisted. "I was afraid that you would never come back after last summer, and we really need to hear the things you have to say about God. I don't have much money and I have to watch every penny, but I know that giving you this $5 is the right thing to do. I want to help you carry on with your work."

That first summer night in the town with its crowd of angry young men was the worst experience I've had in all these years of street preaching. But speaking God's word will not always be easy. There will be those who hate us, those who are drunk, those who are envious. As I preached that night, we must try to return our enemies' hate with love. Hard as it may be sometimes, we must have patience. I thank God for giving me the strength not to take a swing at the drunken young men. What kind of a Christian witness would I have been had I given in to the itch of temptation?

The young men with their anger and their drinking come and go, but the older people with their generosity and their thirst for the word of God endure. Even if the widow lady's kindness were my only motivation to keep on street preaching, I would persevere. But I have many more memories that spur me on — like the story of the man who wanted to shoot himself.

I met this man on a bright August day in Breathitt County, in a little place off Highway 30, not far from a town called Quicksand. It was an unlikely time and place for us to preach. Most days we stopped preaching around 5:00 so we could have dinner, then resume preaching around 7:00 in the evening, and it was very close to 5:00 — time for our break. And we didn't usually preach in such tiny places. This spot couldn't even be called a hamlet. It had only about five or six houses, and normally we liked to have at least twelve or so.

For some strange reason, I decided to stop there anyway. We sang and preached for about 20 minutes. While we were doing so, I noticed a man in a beat-up old Chevrolet going past us. He would slow down and listen for a moment, then move on. But in just a minute or two, he'd be back. I guess maybe he drove by half a dozen times in the course of that 20 minutes.

When we were getting ready to leave, the man in the Chevrolet got out of his car and spoke to us. What he had to say still rings in my mind when I think about God's mysterious ways:

"You know, I need to thank you for coming here and preaching today," he said. "I came past here to do something till I saw you all."

"Where were you going?" I asked him.

"Well, I was going out to shoot myself," he admitted. He pulled a pistol from his pocket to prove his point. "I was going out here and just get rid of all my problems.''

I asked the man what was troubling him.

"You know, I've got a lot of sorrows," he told me. "My wife has done left me. We got four children and she took them all up to Dayton, Ohio. This last weekend, I went on up there to see if I could find them. The kids were just playing around any old place up there, and when I got into the house where they're staying, my wife's in bed with another man.''

A look of anguish passed over the man's face. He took a deep breath, and went on.

"I just went crazy. I thought maybe I'd kill that fellow, but then I thought, no, I'll just run. I ran all the way back home. I've just been stewing within myself to see what I am going to do about this. I finally decided today that I was going out and commit suicide. That's where I was going right now when I heard you all preaching and decided to stop and listen to what you had to say.''

"What are you going to do now?" I asked.

"I don't know, but I reckon I just forgot about how much that Jesus man suffered for me. I reckon I can take a little bit more if I think of Him.''

I never saw this man again. I hope and pray that he went on to make some kind of life for himself, that he found a way to continue to be a father to his children. But I do know that for one short moment that August afternoon, we stood between him and his own death. God won, and the man lived.

I don't go out into these hills and hollers expect-

ing to save lives, but I'm glad that God could use
me as an instrument in staving off this man's suicide.
And I do believe that our preaching improves the
lives of those who hear it. I believe this because so
many of our listeners tell us, with deep gratitude,
how much our preaching means to them.

In a small trailer park where we once preached,
a young man came up to me and said, "You know,
this is the kind of preaching that I really appreciate.
I heard it way down the road and I came up to be
close and listen." I don't think this young man went
to church much, but his hunger for the word of God
was evident.

"You know," he told me, "you made God sound
so good. Too often we get preachers 'round these
parts that like beating a man down. They beat him
down so bad that not even a fly would light on him.
But I felt good after you got done. I felt like I really
wanted to be with God despite the fact that I know
I got my faults."

I'm sure the preachers this man referred to don't
mean to "beat a man down." The last thing these
people need is to be beaten down any further. Their
hard lives have done enough of that.

"If I can be helpful to God in giving just a little
hope, just a little of His light to these mountain people," I thought, "I'll be more than satisfied."

That night, as we closed our preaching with final
prayers, I thanked God that we had been found
worthy in some small way to be a part of His amazing kingdom and His wondrous works.

The Possible Dream

Parents, do not irritate your children or they will lose heart.

— Colossians 3:21

Too many of the teenagers in Appalachia are angry. Often their anger is just the public side of their heartbreak and despair. At the Christian Appalachian Project, it's our job to show them that they can expect more out of life than sorrow, disappointment, and frustration.

Sometimes they find our message of hope hard to believe. Considering the misery they've seen in their short lives, I don't blame them. But I do try to show them another side to the story.

I remember a boy named Bobby, whom I met on a boating trip CAP sponsored a few years back. I had arranged to take 25 young men, representing every faction present in these mountains — white, black, Catholic, Protestant, handicapped, and more — on a 1,000-mile river trip.

I knew to expect some problems. But I hadn't expected to find myself in a near fist-fight with a boy named Bobby.

Bobby was almost 17, strong and defiant. He had plenty of experience in fighting and brawling. He wanted to let everyone know that he was tough — very tough. One evening, as we were all getting ready for bed, some of the boys asked if they could call home. I said yes, but asked them to wait until morning. They agreed — except Bobby. The other boys informed me that he had left the boat and was making his phone call.

I was tired, wanting only to sit quietly and talk with God for a few minutes at the end of a long day. When Bobby got back on the boat, I told him to get to sleep and that we would discuss his disobedience in the morning.

But Bobby wasn't about to take orders from me. "I'm going back down to finish my call. I got cut off before I was done."

"No, you are not," I said.

"Well, who do you think can stop me?" the boy shouted.

"I will," I said.

Bobby was wiry and hard and primed to fight. "I'm coming through you, and I'll hurt you real bad!" he yelled.

"Bobby, you're a tough kid. Anybody would find you hard to handle. But I'm a grown man and I'm not afraid," I told him.

"I'll hit you so hard you'll cry!" he answered.

"Well, I'll tell you one thing," I said, "I won't hit you back."

Bobby stared at me, defiant and unbelieving. "What do you mean, you won't hit me back?" he finally demanded.

"If I wanted to, Bobby, I could break your ribs with one punch," I said. (I weigh 270 pounds and am over six feet tall.) "But I didn't come on this trip to fight with boys. I came here so that you could have a good time. I'm here to love and to care, not to hit and hurt."

It's amazing how quiet 24 teenagers can be when they want to be, I thought. For what seemed like a long time, their attentive silence surrounded Bobby and me. The only sound came from the river lapping gently at the shore.

Bobby yelled out his frustration. "It isn't fair! You have to fight! That's the only way I know how to settle this!"

I went over to Bobby. I put an arm around him and led him to his cot. "Lay down and try to sleep. You can call home in the morning."

"Call home, hell," he said through gritted teeth. "I'm going home in the morning."

Though it was past midnight, I didn't feel like sleeping. I sat in a chair on the upper deck of the houseboat, looking at the stars and wishing I could have the wisdom of the God who made them.

After about half an hour, Bobby came over to me. "I can't sleep. Can we talk?" he asked.

We went ashore and sat down on two wooden crates, right underneath the pay phone that had caused all the controversy.

I asked Bobby why he was so angry. He said everyone in his life hassled him: his mom, his brothers, his teachers.

"What about your dad?" I asked.

"Yeah, him, too, sometimes, but not often."

"When he does give you trouble, what does he do?" I had a feeling I already knew the answer.

"He hits me. He's the strongest man I've ever seen. I don't want to cross him. He's the only man I'm afraid of!"

"Do you really think your dad would hurt somebody?" I asked.

"I don't think it, I know it," Bobby told me. "He put my uncle in the hospital with his bare fists. We tried to paint over the bloodstains but they still showed through. Mom had to put panelling up so we couldn't see them any more."

"How about your brother? Do you fight a lot?" I asked.

"We used to, all the time. But we got in a terrible fight over a pickup truck. I told him I was leaving with it and he tried to stop me. I ran over him and broke his leg. Then my dad found out, he beat me up one side and down the other. I thought I would die. Since then, my brother and me don't fight much. My brother knows that I mean business and I know that my dad does, too."

It was clear that violence ruled Bobby's world. Apparently, love had nothing to do with family life for this youngster.

"How about friends? Do you have any friends at all?" I asked him.

"Yeah, but they don't last," Bobby said. "Just last month my best friend drowned swimming in the river that runs past our house. Then a girl I liked, she got killed. She used to come and see me and we'd talk about her problems. Her stepfather put big welts on her with a two-by-four. We talked about running away, but we didn't get a chance. She was coming up the railroad tracks to see me. Her foot got wedged in the tracks and the train couldn't stop in time."

Bobby's eyes filled with tears. I put my arms around him. He cried and cried. I don't know how long we stayed there like that. When I took him back to his bed, it was 2:30 a.m.

Bobby stayed with our boat trip. I don't know what happened to him after that. There are so many youngsters like him, and, as a human being, I can't follow up as I would like to in every case. That's one of the reasons CAP depends so heavily on the help of volunteers and donors who make it possible for us to reach — and reach out to — more people.

However Bobby's story ended, I do know that it is not unique. Many of the mountain youngsters know little else besides violence and tragedy. They've been raised in homes seething with frustration and anger. Often they're exposed very early to drug and alcohol abuse.

Some of the mountain parents tell their children not to bother with school, that it's a waste of time.

Even the most naturally gifted children can't fight that message of hopelessness all alone.

That's why our CAP Teen Centers are so very important. We want to show these youngsters that life is more than fighting, gambling, and drinking. We want to show them bright horizons beyond the gloomy, smoky rooms they grew up in.

We want to show them that God loves each of them and wants to see them prosper.

And if the teenagers' response to our centers is any indication, God is helping us get the message across.

Take our center in Rockcastle County as an example. When we opened it, we set a goal to have 20 teens actively involved in Teen Center programs and 40 more using the center as a recreational facility.

By the time we reached our goal deadline, however, we had far exceeded our highest hopes. More than 60 teens were involved in programs of one kind or another — tutoring, counseling, music lessons, sports, facility improvement, rap sessions. More than *340* had enjoyed the recreational possibilities of the Center — over eight times as many as we had originally hoped!

That says a lot about the crying need of these youngsters for a little love, a little companionship, a little fun in their lives.

Of course, nearly all teenagers go through rough times as they grow toward adulthood. That's reflected in the national statistics. Teenagers have a higher suicide rate than any other age group. They're struggling with the twin scourges of drug and alcohol abuse. They're getting pregnant out of wedlock at an alarming rate.

The teenagers in Kentucky have all those problems — plus a lot more. Poverty. Isolation. No part-time jobs to be had. Next to no recreational facilities to enjoy. And they are saddled with a tradition of illiteracy and disregard for education. In their region, nearly 50% of all high school students drop out before graduation, the highest percentage anywhere in America.

The kids are up against bad odds. If nothing else, at least CAP's Teen Centers give them an opportunity to come by after school with friends, have a soda, play some pool or ping pong, listen to some music.

That's how we draw the teenagers in, by offering fun and companionship. Then, once they're here, we try to do more. First and foremost, we build relationships. Our Teen Center counselors do their best to get to know each teenager who visits — to develop a rapport and let the kids know that we're here to talk if they need us.

Then we introduce other possibilities, like peer-group rap sessions, where teenagers share their views about issues like drugs, relationships, and moral values. We take them on field trips to local colleges and help them fill out applications. We provide tutoring and counseling. We broaden their horizons with activities like music lessons and aerobics and photography.

So, among the ping-pong and foosball tables, the too-loud tape player and the small library, the board games and the T.V.-watching area, some very serious business is going on. We are fighting for these children's lives.

On good days, I believe we are winning.

At the Rockcastle County Teen Center alone, we have some proud accomplishments.

We've helped several teens decide to stay in school. We've helped several fourteen-year-old girls decide not to get married. We've helped a seventeen-year-old boy begin to deal with his alcoholism. We've walked with dozens of kids through personal and family problems too numerous to count.

One of the boys who's a "regular" at the Rockcastle Center told the center manager, Ike Adams, that the center reminds him of a garden.

"Why's that?" Ike asked him, expecting to hear that — since the place usually needs a little cleaning up — it seemed like a garden because it required frequent weeding.

"It's 'cause you all keep planting little seeds in people's minds, and I keep watching them grow," he told Ike. "Every time I come in here, I feel like I've been watered and fertilized."

That's one of the nicest compliments a CAP program has ever received. And I hope we can keep our garden growing and thriving at all three CAP Teen

Centers. These children certainly need us.

I wish the Teen Centers had been here when Bobby was struggling to grow up — or another boy I met around the same time, a fellow named Eddie.

I met Eddie on a summer boat trip, too. One day as I sat on the front deck of the boat in a rare moment of quiet, Eddie sidled up to me. He was about 12 years old at the time, thin and shy. He had a bad stutter. He looked very unhappy.

"Father," he said to me, "what do you do when even your mother hates you?"

I was a bit shocked by his question, but I assumed that it reflected the usual teenager-parent power struggle.

"Eddie, surely your mother doesn't hate you," I said confidently. "Just because she makes you do things you don't want to do — that happens to all of us. What makes you think she hates you?"

"When I was nine years old, she got mad at me and took me to the bathroom and stuck my head down in the toilet bowl and tried to drown me," the boy said simply.

My easy confidence was shattered. I had never heard a story like this one before.

He continued. "When I made a fuss in the bathroom, my grandmother came in to see what was wrong. She stopped my mother and took me home with her. The next day a social worker came to talk to me and we went to court. The judge took me away from my mother and I lived with my grandmother."

"Do you still live with her?" I asked.

"No, she got sick in the winter and they had to take her into one of those nursing homes. So now I live with a foster family."

"What about your father, Eddie? Does he come to see you?" Surely there must be a ray of sunshine *somewhere* in this sad child's life!

"My father is dead," Eddie said. "My dad and my mom had a big argument. They was making a lot of noise and a man who was a friend of ours came to the house. He and my dad got into a big fight and he hit my dad on the head with a bottle full of whiskey. It knocked my dad plumb out and he never did come to. He died two weeks after that."

I shook my head. "What did your mother do then?"

"She married the other man less than a month later and she never has come to see me." Eddie started to cry. "She still doesn't want to see me. Why does she hate me? I don't hate her."

I looked at the boy. I knew he didn't do well in school. He had few friends. He would probably go from one foster home to another. In another week I would never see him again.

I told Eddie that people would love him. Friends would come when he needed them. Be open to them. Let them love you, I pleaded.

I have thought of and prayed for Eddie many times since that July day on the Kentucky River. My only hope for him lies with God. He alone can give a satisfactory answer to a boy whose father has been killed in a drunken brawl and whose mother tries to drown him in a toilet bowl.

I certainly couldn't.

Thank God, not every teenager in Appalachia has a story like Bobby's or Eddie's. They do face poverty and the trouble that comes with it, a lack of opportunity, and a dearth of hope. But in spite of all their problems, they still try. They are bright and loving and they want to make a better world for themselves.

The kids at the Wheelwright Teen Center have shown us what they can do when given a chance. To raise money for the National Kidney Foundation, they collected $175.00 worth of pull-tabs from aluminum soda cans for recycling. (That's a *lot* of pull-tabs!) The Rockcastle Teen Center kids completed $5,000 worth of maintenance and repair work to their center. Center manager Ike Adams says the list of their accomplishments is endless, "but it includes completion of a new study room, new carpet, new paint, new furniture, a new music room, and lots of cleaning and sprucing up."

They are wonderful, vibrant young people with the same kinds of hopes and dreams as any other teenagers. But, in many cases, the obstacles between them and their cherished goals loom much larger than they do for their counterparts outside of Appalachia.

I'll never forget a story told by Heidi Anne Porter,

who, as a CAP volunteer from Alaska, has worked with Emergency Assistance and managed the Martin Youth Center. Heidi told of the "culture shock" she experienced upon first coming to eastern Kentucky.

"When I went on my first home visit, my immediate reaction was, 'I want to go home.' I was frightened by what I saw." Heidi had never witnessed the poverty and degradation that are so common here. What made her stay?

"I can remember one home visit like it was yesterday," this dedicated young woman says. "A young boy was so excited. He ran back to get this beat-up old tape player and out of a tiny little speaker came the song, 'The Impossible Dream.' It struck a very disturbing chord within."

Heidi does not believe that the dreams of the young in Appalachia should be impossible. I don't either. With God's help, and with our hard work, maybe they won't be.

100,000 Corn-Husk Flowers

Set to work, then, and may Yahweh be with you!

— I Chronicles 22:16

Making a flower out of corn-husks may not seem like a big deal to most people.

Nor is working at a fast-food restaurant considered the pinnacle of success by most people in modern-day America.

But, for the workers at CAPrice Industries here in eastern Kentucky, making corn-husk flowers and serving soft drinks can be very great accomplishments indeed.

CAPrice started as a "sheltered workshop" in 1979 — a place where mentally, emotionally, and physically handicapped people could learn to work and live productive lives.

At first, the corn-husk flowers were just a by-product of the training process. Producing them was not intended to be an economic venture for the Christian Appalachian Project.

But the corn-husk flowers have become very popular. (So have other products made by our

Christmas Ridge division, like our brooms, bird-houses, Memorial Day crosses, and Christmas wreaths. Making and selling these items provides a significant number of full-time, part-time, and seasonal jobs for the local people.)

Today, we ship over 100,000 corn-husk flowers each year from our CAPrice workshop in Stanford, Kentucky. We could not possibly keep up with the demand for these unique, hand-made flowers without the dedication and skill of our CAPrice workers.

We're grateful to have them. And they are grateful to have these jobs.

At CAPrice, most workers have never had a job before. Their education has been spotty at best. Many of them have spent their lives shut off from the world because of their handicaps and their poverty. They had no reason to believe that the future held much in store for them.

When I think about these folks, I try to imagine what it would be like to be young and healthy and full of life, but to feel that you have been sentenced to be "different" because of a disability. . . to know that you will never share in the normal life of your brothers and sisters.

It doesn't seem fair, does it? Perhaps our CAPrice workers make such excellent employees because they've waited so long to be given a chance to prove themselves. Even if they wouldn't put it in words exactly this way, they want to be productive. They want to be independent. They want to be just like everybody else — to have jobs and homes and people to love.

In addition to our corn-husk flower sheltered workshop, CAPrice offers training programs in the food service and housekeeping fields at its Somerset, Kentucky facility. Here workers learn skills that can be transferred to jobs in restaurants, hotels, and other settings. A growing tourist trade in Somerset has meant a boom in the local hospitality industry, creating job openings for CAPrice graduates like Bernice and Pam.

Bernice is one of our Somerset success stories. Deaf and mentally retarded, Bernice trained in the housekeeping program at CAPrice until she was ready to take a job at the Holiday Inn. A CAPrice counselor took the job in Bernice's place for the first two weeks of training, then accompanied Bernice on the job, teaching her and interpreting for her until she knew the routine. A valued employee of the Holiday Inn, Bernice lives with her husband, Danny, whom she met when they were both making corn-husk flowers at CAPrice. Danny says Bernice keeps their apartment just as clean and sparkling as she does the Holiday Inn. "When I try to help, she kicks me out," Danny says.

"No," laughs Bernice, "he's lazy!"

Danny and Bernice enjoy the freedom of living independently and taking responsibility for having their own home. They are two CAPrice success stories. Pam is another.

In many parts of the United States, fast-food restaurants have a hard time hiring good employees. People don't want to do that kind of work. Even unemployed people sometimes will turn up their nose at these jobs.

But not Pam.

Pam makes french fries and fills soft drink cups and keeps the restaurant's dining area clean. She wanted the job. In fact, the interview frightened her, because the working world was so new to her — and because she so much wanted the job. Now her manager praises her as a terrific employee. Of all the aspects of her job, Pam most enjoys working with people, both co-workers and customers.

Bernice and Pam are just two of the CAPrice graduates who have become productive members of their community. They know the satisfaction of putting in a good day's work, and the pride of earning their own living. CAPrice Industries has turned their lives around, and we hope to do so for more and more of eastern Kentucky's handicapped adults.

But we are also constantly working to bring more jobs to the region for *everyone*. With the collapse of the coal industry, there is not much left in eastern Kentucky. CAP itself provides several hundred jobs through its Christmas Ridge product marketing division and in CAP administration. But several hundred jobs make up little more than a drop in the bucket.

CAP is working with state and local agencies,

citizens groups, and coalitions of local businesspeople to encourage companies to move here and hire our local people. We've had some successes. But we need more, much more.

With the mountains' isolation and rugged terrain, enticing companies to set up shop here takes some doing. And, while our people are ready and willing to work, they often lack the skills and education level required for jobs in manufacturing and technology.

That's another reason our adult literacy and education programs are so very important — and why our efforts with children and teenagers are crucial. Without an educated work force, we can't attract the industry we so desperately need, if Appalachia is ever to escape the cruel grip of economic depression.

I believe we can do it. I've dedicated my life to trying. I want to see full employment for the wonderful people who have struggled to eke out a livelihood in these mountains. I want to see them fulfilled as human beings. I want to see them set free of poverty's painful chains.

We start with a few corn-husk flowers. Soon we're making 100,000. That's one story of hope. I tell the mountain folk, let's create some more success stories. If Bernice can do it, if Pam can do it, we can all do it.

And we must.

Peace on Earth and Mercy Mild

In hope, we already have salvation.

— Romans 8:24

I wish Christmas didn't have to come in winter.

You're probably thinking that's a pretty strange notion. I've been thinking it for years.

You see, I think of Christmas as such a joyous time. We hope for the best. We expect the noble. We want to re-create childhood memories of happy holidays with a loving family — or, if we never had such wonderful times, we want to have them now.

But for so many of the poor in Appalachia, Christmas is a desolate time. It is a time of sharp winds and bitter coldness seeping through the thin walls of rickety houses, of burn-outs as poor families try desperately to stay warm. It is a time of even greater isolation and numbing boredom for those who have no work and no money for diversions — not even a radio or a T.V. It is a time when the chronic ailments that haunt these people flare up to make everyday life even more painful.

In winter, and at Christmas, the people dream

more but receive little. They hunger and go unfed. The children know that other children, somewhere else, in a magic land they hear about from a distance, wake up to shiny new toys — fabulous inventions, really — under a well-dressed Christmas tree.

Here in eastern Kentucky, some of our children get just one used toy for Christmas. And they're grateful for that!

A few hundred miles from here in any direction, people have too much: too much food, too much drink, too much in the way of material things. A few days before Christmas in 1988, a Washington, D.C. newspaper ran a story about a man who was buying a Mercedes convertible for his wife for Christmas.

It was to be the fourth in the couple's collection of Mercedes automobiles. The new car would cost $64,000, give or take a few dollars.

I hear stories like these. I know they are not uncommon in certain parts of our nation.

Then I look at the face of a child whose Christmas stocking is pitifully empty. . . at the faces of parents who hurt because they cannot give their children more. And I have to admit, the contrast between the man with the Mercedes and the poor of Appalachia makes me angry sometimes.

But that's when I am reminded that Christmas still brings love and hope and good news, no matter what's under the tree, to all whose hearts are open to Christ. Often the mountain people themselves forcefully remind me that the baby Jesus is the true focus of Christmas.

CAP gives out Christmas baskets to needy families in our operating area. Last year we gave out over 2,000. We ask recipients to come to central distribution points so we can fulfill one of their requests — to have an interdenominational worship service to celebrate the coming of Jesus and to thank God for the gifts we are about to receive.

Many among this year's congregation thanked me for the worship service. Many say, "This is more important than our Christmas baskets." One lady came up to me with a special question.

"Who do we thank for the fact that you are a priest, a minister of God?" she asked.

"Do you mean who do you thank for the things in your Christmas basket?" I said.

"No, I mean who do we thank because you brought us Jesus?" she replied. "You can get what's in the basket from a store, but what you gave us was the notion that God loves us and we are His family. That's a notion we seldom hear."

The mountain folk embrace the Word of God with enthusiasm. They need to hear that they are loved. They need to know that Jesus was born, lived, and died for them. More than most people, they need to feel the meaning of Christmas in their hearts.

At the same time, it is a joy for all of us at CAP to see that our friends and neighbors get a few nice material things at Christmastime. That's why the

Christmas Basket Program is so important to us.

Across America, families who have come to know CAP's work help sponsor the Christmas baskets. Sometimes they donate money to help us purchase gifts. More often, we give them information about what a particular family needs, and they select, purchase, and send the gifts to us. The sponsoring families tell us that filling a CAP Christmas basket makes their own Christmas especially meaningful.

What goes in a Christmas basket? Well, they're custom-made for each family. All the baskets contain ample food for a wonderful Christmas meal and enough for a few days afterwards. There's almost always clothing and a hand-made ornament from school children or elderly active in CAP programs. And when the family has children, we try to include school supplies and some special toys, knowing full well that many children will receive no others.

Our Christmas Basket Program has been blessed by the efforts of families across the country, and by the work of a very special man named Father Giles Hayes and his students from The Delbarton School in Morristown, New Jersey.

Every year, for the last seven years, boys from Delbarton have gathered money and gifts for the Christmas baskets in their home town. Then about 20 of them accompany Father Hayes, and their bounty of gifts, to eastern Kentucky to help assemble and distribute the Christmas baskets.

For the most part, the boys from Delbarton have never seen poverty like ours before. They come from an upper middle class area, from stable families where it is assumed that they will go on to college and fulfilling careers. The tuition at Delbarton is $7,000 a year. To say these young men experience culture shock in eastern Kentucky is an understatement.

But they make the most of their time here, truly bringing joy to people who have so little.

Energetic, strong, and healthy, the Delbarton boys don Santa Claus caps and race around the CAP warehouse, sorting, packing, and arranging heavy Christmas baskets — they're actually boxes — for pick-up. When families cannot come to get their baskets, the Delbarton gang takes to the road. One lucky young man gets to dress up in full Santa Claus regalia to delight the children who have never seen a department store Santa — who might have thought Santa would forget all about them.

Their visits to Appalachia change the Delbarton students' outlook on the world. To Father Hayes, their college counselor, it's a crucial step in their learning process.

"What we're doing down here is only a tiny Band-aid," Father Hayes told *The New York Times* recently, "but maybe 20 years down the road, when the Delbarton kids are corporate lawyers or bankers, they'll be in positions and have the desire to break the cycle of poverty."

This year, at least one of the boys started thinking about volunteering because of his trip to eastern Kentucky. "I'm thinking about going into engineering," Sean Gallagher said. "But now I'm thinking about doing a year or two of this kind of work first. Students who come down here come back with real positive things to say. They come back more serious. They come back more grown up."

So the mountain folk give these young men a precious gift in return for their generosity — the gift of compassion for their fellow human beings.

The mountain folk *want* to give, and they do. They give of themselves in volunteer services to CAP. They give to each other in cooperation and caring, sharing the little they have with others in time of trouble. Often they wish they had more to give, like a lady named Juanita I talked to this Christmas.

"I'm grateful for the Christmas basket," she said, "Lord knows we wouldn't have much of anything without it." Juanita's husband John has not been able to work since a coal car fell on him in a mine some years ago. Though she's only 40, Juanita herself suffers from a chronic heart ailment. They have four children.

"But one time I'd like to be able to go into a store and buy just one present for each of my kids. Just one present I picked out and paid for myself," she explained wistfully.

I wanted to hand Juanita some money and say, "Here, go and do it. You deserve it. Your children deserve it." Of course, I couldn't do that, and she wouldn't accept it if I did. But it makes my heart ache to hear a mother say that all she wants for Christmas is — just once — to be able to select one gift for each of her four children.

Juanita has never been able to enjoy that simple kind of giving.

And yet, in a mighty city just a short hop away by plane, a man gave his wife a $64,000 car to put in the driveway with their other three $64,000 cars.

I wonder what might move that man to share some of his bounty with the poor of Appalachia. Maybe if he knew what I know, if he had seen what I've seen.

Maybe if he knew the story of the man with two burlap sacks.

I met the man a few years ago, during one of our most severe snows ever. Yes, it would be a white Christmas. But in these mountains, it would mean more suffering, not just more beauty. I didn't welcome the snow.

I was leaving our church at McKee after Christmas services, driving back to CAP headquarters in Lancaster. I saw the man thumbing on the side of the highway. He had a bundle under his arm. I picked him up and asked him where he was going.

"Sand Gap," he said, naming a community about six miles away.

"What are you doing going there on Christmas Day in such bad weather?" I asked.

"We don't have any fuel at home," he said, unfolding his bundle to reveal two burlap sacks. "I hear there's a big tree that blew down over at Sand Gap. If the branches are rotten I can break 'em up and fill these sacks with wood. Then I'll try to hitch another ride back home. The children are cold. We need some firewood bad."

For a moment, I didn't believe my ears. Could it really be that this family's cherished Christmas hope was to fill two sacks with wood so they might have a little warmth? Could this really be happening in America?

I let the man off at Sand Gap. I saw him a few weeks later. He told me that he had gotten the wood and that by evening he and his family had been able to get warm, huddled around the fireplace.

I was glad. But his story touched my heart, as did the story of another lady who was very excited about the holiday one year.

I asked her if she planned to give her family something special this Christmas.

She beamed. "Yes," she said proudly, "A cake! *With icing on it!*"

Imagine. This poor mountain woman had scrimped and saved to buy the ingredients for a cake — with icing. To her and to her family, this would be a very special treat indeed.

To most people in our wealthy nation, a simple cake would be a paltry Christmas gift. In a way, I think this woman was lucky. Because she had so little, she retained a sense of joy in simple things, and she knew the real pleasure of giving.

The lady with the cake knew the true spirit of Christmas — the spirit that has nothing to do with Christmas lights and rampant commercialism and billions upon billions of dollars spent in gifts to overwhelm both children and adults.

Now I'm no Scrooge. Far from it. Every year I deck out my little house with Christmas decorations and candles and wreaths. I don't miss the chance to celebrate this great festival.

But I also don't forget my neighbors and friends who can't buy a single strand of lights for a Christmas tree, or a single, simple gift for their own children. I can't forget that there are children in these hollers who have never seen a Christmas light or even a picture of Santa Claus.

And I try not to lose sight of God's great gift to all of us at Christmastime — his Son.

Because of the power of our Lord Jesus Christ, my Christmas in 1988 was my best ever, even though I spent a good part of Christmas Day in jail.

First, I preached a Christmas Eve service in a town 60 miles away. I got home at 2:30 a.m. On Christmas morning I got up early to bring Christmas to another church — a chapel in a trailer, actually — 30 miles from my home.

The people would not have had Mass in their humble chapel had I not made time to drive those 30 miles. They thanked me for bringing Christmas to them. And then I was on the road again, on my way to the jail in Lee County, some distance away.

A man named Paul, my friend of more than 20 years, was imprisoned there. I believe he is innocent. Nevertheless, Paul was in jail. I arrived there at around 1:00. Paul wasn't expecting me.

"Why are you here?" he asked, startled.

"To bring Christmas," I replied.

Paul's eyes filled with tears.

His wife and kids and neighbors came to join us. The jailer kindly offered us the use of an empty cell. Our altar was a metal table bolted to the floor. We were surrounded by prison bars. Children hung off the bunks. I said Mass in the jail cell.

In some ways, the cold, gray jail cell seemed like the worst possible place to celebrate Mass on Christmas Day. But really, what could be more appropriate? Who needs God's Word more than those in prison — whether they are innocent or guilty of the crimes they are accused of?

Paul was overjoyed. "I do believe this may be the best Christmas of my life," he said, "because I have come to appreciate my friends and God."

I left the jail for my 100-mile drive home. I had promised to visit some people and they were still waiting for me. I got my first meal of the day at 5:00 p.m., when a family I was visiting gave me leftover turkey and trimmings. It tasted very good indeed.

My Christmas Day ended around 9:00 that evening. I went home to my empty little house, and I have to admit I felt a little sorry for myself. "I'm tired and worn out," I thought. "My own family is 200 miles away. I can't be with them. I can't enjoy the grandnieces and nephews. I can't be with my brother who is dying. Here I am, far away from all of them, on top of a mountain, and all alone, exhausted by Christmas. What is this all about?"

Then I remembered the joy of the congregation in the trailer...the look on Paul's face when I arrived at the jail...the kindness of the lady who gave me dinner and welcomed me with warm Kentucky hospitality. And I realized that this had really been the best Christmas of my life.

What Christmas means to me is the birth of hope. I sing the old Christmas songs with joy. I believe in their message. I have staked my life on it.

From the Top of the Mountain

There is nothing I cannot do in the One who strengthens me.

— Philippians 4:13

In the summer of 1946, when the Bishop sent me to eastern Kentucky, I didn't want to go.

My father was in the hospital with a crushed leg. I was the oldest of 11 children, and I believed I should stay and work to help the family. The Bishop disagreed. I obeyed.

That summer of 1946, I fell in love with a land and its people.

What did I find here that fascinated me so?

It wasn't the poverty, the rotten houses, hungry kids, or litter-filled hollers. It wasn't the downright desolation of the place.

It was because I saw what eastern Kentucky *could* be.

It could be one of the most spectacularly beautiful places in the world. With its mineral and timber wealth, it did not need to be poor, not if people worked together with honesty and justice.

And the people here — well, their forefathers, our early American pioneers, had been some of the most creative, dynamic people ever to grace this continent. The people could recapture that pioneer spirit. They could make this land flower, given half a chance to escape the yoke of poverty.

Why did I focus on the promise of Appalachia, instead of being repelled by its sad reality? I think my upbringing had something to do with it.

I was born on January 1, 1924, in Newport, Kentucky — not a wealthy part of the world then or now, but not Appalachia, either — to a young couple who were eager to have children. They wanted to experience God's love and God's gifts of life to the fullest. They knew they would have to work hard and sacrifice and struggle. They were far from well-to-do. But love ruled them, and love ruled our household.

When I was 18 months old, our family moved to Highland Heights, Kentucky, to a small farm. My father was a carpenter. During the Depression, he worked for the WPA. At night he went door to door, selling Watkins Products. He picked up other carpentry work when he could.

My parents and my brothers and sisters and I also ran our little 10-acre farm. We raised chickens, pigs and cows. We worked hard, but we had a good life. We were rich in the love of each other and of God.

I attended Newport Catholic High School, then

went to St. Gregory's Seminary in Washington, Ohio and St. Mary's of the West Seminary in Norwood, Ohio. Finally I did my graduate study at Catholic University in Washington, D.C. During these years of education and training, I had my life-changing summer of 1946 in eastern Kentucky. I was ordained to the priesthood on June 4, 1949. I served one happy year as a teacher at my alma mater, Newport Catholic High School, at St. Bernard's Parish in Dayton, Kentucky.

Then the Bishop told me I was to be in charge of a parish—an extraordinarily responsible position for such a young and inexperienced priest. He told me I was to go to eastern Kentucky, that I would be responsible for all the Catholics in a four-county area.

I was excited and flattered. I asked the Bishop what my church would be like.

"There is no church," he told me. "Not yet."

That was all right, I thought, I could cope with that. "How about the rectory?"

"There's no rectory, either," he said.

I knew I was in for an interesting time of it from that moment on.

In the region assigned to me, there was only a handful of Catholics. It was now up to me to find some ways to serve them and to draw more of the mountain people into the fold.

I have been here ever since.

I was surprised by the Bishop's decision, but not

unduly alarmed by the prospect lying ahead of me. Maybe I was suffering from youthful over-optimism. I prefer to think I have my parents to thank for my willingness to take on this challenge. They never backed away from challenge or conflict. I grew up thinking that their courageous, sacrifice-filled way of life was the ordinary way to be. I assumed everyone was like that.

Later in life, I learned that everyone is not. But I do believe that we all have in us the potential to do great things in the Lord's name. The people I have known through the Christian Appalachian Project have proved me right more times than I can count — the mountain people we serve, the CAP staff members, and the thousands of volunteers who have served CAP since its humble beginnings.

Our volunteers come from all over the nation. They stay with us from a week to several years. Many fall in love with the area, as I did, and they put down roots and build their families here. Others serve our community, then go back out into the world to contribute even more. That's what I think of as the CAP "ripple" effect.

There are many examples of former CAP volunteers who are now serving the Lord in other parts of the world. Recently I was sent to Africa by my diocese, on a fact-finding mission to examine programs serving the poor. There, in Khartoum, Sudan, I met a former CAP volunteer who was setting up a charitable program in this area that has been ravaged by civil war and famine. Inspired by her CAP experiences, another former volunteer left to start a home for children called Bethlehem House. And CAP remembers with pride a former volunteer who has become a Juvenile Court Judge in Louisville, Kentucky, where he is known for his innovative programs to help kids.

The Christian Appalachian Project has changed its volunteers' lives — for the better, I believe — just as they have brought light and love into the dark homes of the poor in eastern Kentucky's hollers.

Over these years, our Project has accomplished a great deal because of the dedication of volunteers and the generosity of donors all across America. The donors — who send us desperately needed funds, clothes, toys, even used cars — have a special place in my heart. I think they are the opposite of the Apostle Thomas.

Why? Well, when Christ came back from the dead, he appeared to the women first and then to Peter. Finally, on Easter night, he appeared to all the apostles except Thomas. They all believed. They told Thomas, but Thomas wouldn't believe. He had to put his finger in the nail scars and his hands in Christ's side. Once he had satisfied his skepticism, Thomas dropped to his knees and said, "My Lord and my God."

Jesus said, "You believe because you can see me. Blessed are those who have not seen and yet believe." Most of our CAP donors are in that second category.

They have never personally witnessed the poverty and misery of Appalachia. But they believe, and they sacrifice in order to help those less fortunate than themselves.

To me, that makes them a real part of the CAP family. Without their loyalty and their generosity, our work for the poor here in Appalachia would be impossible.

A few years back, CAP's magazine, *The Mountain Spirit,* published an interview with me. The editor asked me what I considered my biggest disappointment over the years I've spent with CAP. I had to think about that for a moment.

Certainly there have been sad times and discouraging times. We would be of no use whatsoever to the mountain folk if we were unable to share their pain. But I really have no disappointments. What makes something a disappointment? You wanted it to happen today, and it didn't? Is that a disappointment?

To me, it's not a disappointment or failure when you try to do something and it doesn't work out. Failure means that it didn't exactly achieve your immediate desire. But it might have made something better possible. It might have changed people. It might have paved the way for something more wonderful than you had originally planned.

I get disappointed only when I commit a sin. I am sorry when I fail to do what God wanted me to do — and, since I'm human, this happens all too often. But God's forgiveness is there for all of us. I count on it. I hope our Appalachian people do, too.

What lies ahead for my friends and neighbors here in eastern Kentucky? I don't know. When I drive up the holler to the mountaintop where I live, I see their shacks. In winter, I see the burned-out shells of their modest homes, turned to ashes by a bad heater because they tried to keep warm. In the hollers, you see ruins like these up close, and it's not a pretty sight. You see ancient cars and appliances discarded wherever anyone had the energy to haul them. You're constantly reminded of mistakes and disasters and years of oppression. It robs you of hope. You don't see the far horizon, just forested sides of mountains crowding you in and blocking your view of the sky.

I get to the top of the mountain, and the view opens up before me. I can see the beautiful silhouettes of mountain upon mountain in the distance. I can enjoy the brilliant sunsets and stunning sunrises. I am lucky. I live on top of the mountain. Life looks so very different up here — so much more hopeful, so full of possibility.

My one wish for the Appalachian people is that they, too, might share the view from the top of the mountain — that they will be able to reap its promise and know a new day of light and joy.

I wish this simple wish for my friends. And I believe that, with God's help and our continued commitment, it will come true.

I fell in love in 1946. I am still in love today.

"There is nothing I cannot do in the One who strengthens me." That is my watchword. It is my daily bread.

EPILOGUE

Father Beiting refers to me as a "second generation volunteer." Fair enough, I suppose, since my
parents were volunteers.

During several vacations and miscellaneous
weekends during the summer in the early 1960s, my
parents (with my three brothers, sister, and me in
tow) travelled to Garrard County, Kentucky, to offer their assistance to a young priest. This priest
dreamed of making life for the people of the Appalachian mountains as full of promise as it was for
other Americans. Father Beiting believed then, as
now, that through children one gained the trust of
parents, and that by building trusting relationships,
the Appalachian people would gain the resources they
needed to help themselves out of poverty.

Because of my experience as a child, I have been
asked many times since 1977, when I came to CAP
as a volunteer, what Father Beiting was like back then.

I don't remember.

I remember hearing about Father Beiting, and
finally, I figured out that even back then, Father
Beiting spent so much time on the road that my
recollections of him come closer to resembling a

phantom than a dynamo.

I have a couple of concrete memories, but overall, I remember that he impressed me even when I was only eight years old as a person of incredible compassion and love. In the years since then that impression has been reinforced time and again.

Although my family's involvement with Father Beiting and CAP decreased when I was a teenager, the thought that I might return someday as a volunteer occurred to me occasionally when I was in college.

I like to think that my own motivation and altruism led me to do great things for God and humankind, but in all honesty, I should admit that much of my motivation came from observations of Father Beiting and his dream. Many volunteers will tell you the same thing.

Oh, the original thought, "I'd like to do something for other people," is the vague impetus for all us volunteers, but for those who ended up at CAP, it's Father Beiting who allowed, encouraged, and (in some cases) nagged us into putting hands and feet on his dream that we all embraced.

That triumvirate of allowance, encouragement, and nagging could be a textbook example of people management, if you think about it. For example. . .

In 1978, Marilyn Stefanski was running a child development center in Lancaster, Kentucky, CAP's home base. In the course of home visiting, Marilyn met some severely handicapped children that she was not able to serve at the Sunshine Center. With Father Beiting's permission, she returned to graduate school at the University of Kentucky and obtained a master's degree in special education. As Marilyn was finishing her degree, she began working with several handicapped children in their homes. Out of this involvement grew Parents Are Teachers, CAP's homebound program for handicapped preschoolers. A program that today serves 50 to 60 handicapped children in five counties has grown from the freedom that Marilyn was given to reach out and serve the needs she observed.

When Marilyn told Father Beiting of her dream, he could easily have said, "Marilyn, you're doing good and important work in the Sunshine Center. Please concentrate on that." But he didn't. He used Marilyn's desire to serve handicapped children to make yet another opportunity available to those in need. Today, many of those children have been mainstreamed into regular classrooms; others with more severe handicaps have made the most of the capabilities that God has given them.

Father Beiting encourages through example. For someone who talks as well and as much as he does, Father Beiting finds it much easier to show someone how to do something than tell them. This holds true for anything from painting a fence to dealing with people.

One of the greatest examples he ever gave me happened one day when I was travelling around Floyd

County with him. I was doing research for an article for CAP's magazine, *The Mountain Spirit.* It was a beautiful day in the fall, and Father Beiting had many stops in Floyd, Magoffin, and Johnson counties on our itinerary. I was grateful for the special time with him.

Our first stop of the day was close to Martin, Kentucky, at the home of a lady who had made the acquaintance of one of the volunteers. Her husband had been hospitalized but was coming home in the next couple of days. CAP's Home Repair crew had weatherized the house, but Father Beiting wanted to stop in to take some chairs and his TV stand in order to make the family's home as comfortable as possible.

Naturally, this lady was excited about her husband coming home. He had been away for quite some time and the elderly woman had grown very lonely during his absence. Two visitors were just what she needed to pass the torturously slow time until her husband returned.

As she and Father talked aimlessly about this and that, I grew increasingly nervous. I knew perfectly well (and I knew that Father Beiting knew perfectly well) that people were expecting us in a half dozen places in three counties. He didn't rush, though; he was in no hurry. The most important thing to him was to give this lady some of the time that she needed to share and to talk. Sometimes, if I get annoyed with Father Beiting because he's late for something

(Father Beiting is always late for something) I recall that he's probably talking to and becoming God's presence to someone like this lonely woman, and reflect that we should follow his example and do the same.

The third weapon in Father's management arsenal comes in two styles: verbal and non-verbal. Father Beiting will strongly suggest once that someone needs a visit, a garden needs to be weeded, a letter needs to be written. That's verbal nagging. Non-verbal nagging continues as long as one continues to procrastinate. Father Beiting might not say another word for weeks or months about the task, but you'd better believe that he remembers those suggestions, and that he is likely to bring them up at any given time and ask what progress has been made. This kind of non-verbal nagging, too, produces good results. It boils down to the fact that Father Beiting does not accept less than the best effort from himself and by observing this in him, volunteers are motivated to demand even more of themselves.

You've read a lot in this book about how much Father Beiting has done for this area and for the Appalachian people. I would like to emphasize what many people believe is one of Father Beiting's greatest influences on the area — the thousands of people who have come here to help make his dream a reality and help the people of Appalachia help themselves as they work to change their lives for the better. Hundreds of these volunteers have chosen to make Ap-

palachia their home, put down roots, start families
— taking a vital part in the birth of a strong, vibrant
region.

Nearly all the volunteers and former volunteers
I know will tell you that they came to CAP to give
of themselves and ended up taking away more than
they could ever hope to give. Father Beiting is responsible for much of what people gain.

To the litany of human and economic development programs that we can credit Father Beiting with
starting, we can add an incredible knack for bringing capabilities out of people that they had no idea
were there.

You could fill a good-sized room with the people whose reaction to a request or direction from
Father Beiting was "Who me? I can't do that!"
Somehow he can always tell exactly how much a person can do. He stops just short of pushing hard
enough to discourage a person or to make someone
give up.

Even though I'm not able to discourse poetical-
ly on Father Beiting and his activities nearly 30 years
ago, I do want to share one childhood memory.

It was the dead of summer, and Father Beiting
and the people who were working with him were con-
structing one of the buildings on the campgrounds.
I don't know why, but they were unloading a truck
of bricks or rocks or something in the hot, noonday
sun. I suppose they must have been letting the
younger folks "help," probably trying to get all of

this work done despite a lot of little kids underfoot. Even today, I can remember how hot it was, and how hot the work seemed to be. Before long, the men seemed to be working in shifts. Several would stay on the truck, unloading the brick, and one or two would stop for a drink of water or even a quick dunk in Herrington Lake. All except Father Beiting.

One of the workers commented on how hard Father Beiting was working. Without breaking the rhythm of his work or even looking up, he said, almost to himself, "I can't work hard enough."

In all the years since then, I have heard that line echo through my head. As Father Beiting continues his work, his dream, his contact with people, over and over again I can hear him saying, "I can't work hard enough."

—Margaret Gabriel, Editor
The Mountain Spirit

A Letter from Carmen

I'd like to share with you a letter I received not long ago — a letter that touched and warmed my heart. It's from a young woman who was helped by CAP as a child. Grown now, she had not thought of CAP for years until she saw a piece on television about us. Her thoughtfulness in putting her kind words down on paper more than repay anything we did for her twenty years ago.

I invite you to read Carmen's letter and consider what you might do to help the children of God who live in Appalachia.

— Father Ralph Beiting

Dear Father Beiting,

I very highly doubt that you remember me, for many years have passed since I saw you last, and I was only one of the many children who came to St. Paul's in McKee, Kentucky. I couldn't have been more than six or seven at the time, but I never forgot you.

You looked down at me with your kindness and caring when I was a small girl. Somehow in my young mind I knew that though I was one of many poor children in that area, I was not *just* another child to you. My name was Carmen, Abner then, Scott now. There were five of us children and my mother. My father was almost never around. We tried to scratch a living out of the hillside five miles out of Sand Gap, but I know that there were times we wouldn't have made it if not for the caring and help of the people at St. Paul's. I assume that was all a part of the Christian Appalachian Project then, but as a child I wasn't aware of it.

I remember a lot. I remember a Sister Mary Jo and a car full of food when we had none. I remember a brown crib bed with a teddy bear on the headboard and my mother telling me Sister had brought it for me. She was surprised when I mentioned it years later. She had that bed still, but had thought me too young to have remembered where it came from. Nevertheless, I did remember.

I remember the giving and the people who gave. You people made an impression on me and I believe myself to be a better person for having known you and having experienced the kindness of your works. If you ever get discouraged and wonder if what you are doing really helps the people you're trying to reach, I stand as an example that such caring and help touches more than the bellies and hands of children.

My heart was touched through you and my faith was strengthened. Yes, children have faith and I still believe they are more capable of understanding what

Jesus Christ lived and died for than are many adults. Sometimes it is difficult for them to maintain that faith into adulthood when people turn their eyes and hearts away from the face of a child's poverty. Children do not listen to words so much as they listen to faces, to hands and hearts. To a child, a voice that says, "I care," no matter what the words, and a heart, hands, and eyes that show that caring are more the gospel of the Jesus Christ they know than any words of doctrine.

Perhaps I presume too much. I only know that, as a child, I knew Christ. I knew and understood who He was even before I knew you. I believed then and continue to believe that He sent you and the people working with you to show me that through Him I made a difference, that He loved me and would care for me through those who believed in Him. Perhaps He sends me to you now with this letter to show you that through Him you truly do make a difference in the hearts, minds, and souls of the people you touch. For this one, at the very least, your caring was not in vain.

When I saw the piece about CAP on television last night, a lot of memories came rushing back, memories that might not have been so good were it not for the work you have been doing. It's been close to twenty years now, but I will never forget the man who looked down with caring and love in the face of a child's poverty, any more than I can forget the man who lived for us and died for us, whose

love moved you to touch a child's life, to clothe me
and give me food to eat. Your path is a good one
and as you know, our paths are no more sacred than
the manner of our walking. May you always walk
in a sacred manner.

Peace be with you, Father.

Carmen

(one of the least of His little
ones)

Christian Appalachian Project's bimonthly magazine, *The Mountain Spirit,* will keep you up-to-date on all the doings at CAP as we work to help the people of eastern Kentucky. Also, it contains moving, inspiring stories of people like Cecil and Bernice, Dennis and Serelda. If you would like to subscribe to this publication (or renew your subscription), just complete the order form below.

—————————————————————

THE MOUNTAIN SPIRIT Subscription Order Form

Please enter my one-year subscription to *The Mountain Spirit.* I have enclosed my check, made payable to CAP, for $5.00.

Name _____

Address _____

City _____ State _____ Zip _____

Please return this Order Form, along with your check to: Christian Appalachian Project, 322 Crab Orchard Road, Lancaster, KY 40446

If You'd Like to
Know More About the
Christian Appalachian Project...

For more information about CAP, or for
additional copies of *God Can Move Mountains*,
please write or phone us at our headquarters:

Christian Appalachian Project
322 Crab Orchard Road
Lancaster, KY 40446
(606) 792-3051

Thank you for your interest and support!